DIGITAL
BACON

MAKE YOUR ONLINE PRESENCE IRRESISTIBLY ATTRACTIVE

ALEX RODRIGUEZ

Creative Strategy Tips

Digital BACON
Make Your Online Presence Irresistibly Attractive
First Edition

Published 2014
YMMY Marketing, LLC (ymmymarketing.com)
Creative Strategy Tips (creativestrategytips.com)

This book is not intended to provide legal, financial, nor investment advice. The Author and the Publisher specifically disclaim any liability, loss or risk which is incurred as a consequence, directly or indirectly, of the use and application of any contents of this work.

ISBN 978-0-9906424-0-4
Library of Congress Control Number: 2014914673
1. Business and Economics; 2. Computers: Web; 3. Business: Advertising & Promotion

Written by Alex Rodríguez

Foreword by Chris Brogan

Illustrations by Nathan Rodríguez

Edited by Nicholas Georgandis

Cover design, diagrams, and layout by YMMY Marketing

Some of the links in this book may point to a resource that offers the publisher an affiliate comission per registration or paid account.

Printed in the United States of America

Thank You

To Christ my Lord, who is truly YHWH-Yireh (I believe that's Hebrew for "He will bring home the bacon.")

To Chava, my other half in ways that still surprise me. Te amo. Sin ti no hubiera sido posible.

To Nathan and Seth, my two lifelong dreams, inspirations, and legacies. I do everything for you.

To the Dominican BBS Community (BBSianos). Two decades ago, you showed me how to create long-lasting connections through digital media, and I still owe you so much.

To my parents, siblings, brethren, friends, supporters, partners, and clients. For every inch of confidence you place in me, I receive the strength to run five miles farther.

Contents

FOREWORD
"WHAT ALEX DOESN'T KNOW"
by CHRIS BROGAN

My house smells of bacon as I type these words — real bacon. Alex doesn't know that because he doesn't live here. That would be weird. Well, unless we were a superhero team.

Alex also doesn't know that my own project, *The Owner's Path*, focuses on a solid framework to help people improve their personal leadership, and thus build stronger influence and impact. The framework that I use isn't the same as the BACON framework in this book, but there are some similarities. Alex doesn't know this because he doesn't live near me nor work with me directly.

I'm guessing Alex doesn't know much about making something go "viral," at least in the way that clients tend to use the word. Replace "viral" with "magic" or "bitten by a radioactive spider." Alex doesn't know that because he actually knows how to make things happen the real way. The BACON way.

Really, when you get right down to it, Alex doesn't know how to diet, because this book is **fat** with ideas, concepts, and work for you to do. You will **not** lose mental weight on the BACON book diet. Digital or not, this BACON book is **FAT**.

And what you don't know — yes, I mean *you* — is probably somewhere in this book... at least if what *you* don't know deals with how to attract and keep the right kinds of clients and customers. But don't lose too much sleep about that. Alex knows. And he will help.

I'd write more, but my house smells of bacon as I type these words.

And besides, you have a book to read.

Chris Brogan
CEO Owner Media Group
and author of *The Freaks Shall Inherit the Earth*

Introduction

"Millions of dollars in sales in just a few days ..."

*"Double and triple percentage lifts
in audience numbers ..."*

*"Record-breaking number of pre-sales
in a launch campaign ..."*

Would you like to end this year being able to claim achievements like the ones above for *your* company?

If you're like most people in charge of promoting a business, nothing would make you happier. You have probably heard of companies and agencies deploying successful digital efforts and achieving results like these, but might be wondering how it's even possible.

Believe me ... it's absolutely possible. How do I know?

The above examples are results I have personally helped my clients achieve, and I've done so by implementing the formula I am going to share with you in this book. By the time you finish reading, you will have learned the process to present your offer in an *irresistibly attractive* manner, by promoting your products and services to a large audience in a powerful manner, and securing a fantastic return on investment (ROI) for your company.

You'll notice I used the words "irresistibly attractive" above. I use this phrase heavily throughout this book, because I can imagine that this is the effect you want to cause on your prospective customers when you present your business's offer. You want a strong pulling force in *your* direction, one which they simply cannot fight against.

Sort of like what *bacon* does to the average person.

Unless you're a vegetarian, everything about bacon drives a person absolutely insane. The color and crispy/chewy texture, the sizzle, the smell, and of course, the flavor. Everything about bacon is perfectly aligned to make you salivate, while your mind fires  on all pistons just imagining when you can have your next blissful encounter with that very special and unique palate-teaser. Someone once described the flavor of bacon as "angels frolicking on the tip of your tongue." Sounds pretty accurate to me!

You see, bacon isn't simply another member of the *meat* family, even though it is obviously a meat product. When you think of meat, what comes to mind are steaks, pork chops, ribs, etc. However, when you think about BACON, something much more rare and special ... something **awesome** comes to mind. You never think of regular old meat, but rather an incomparably unique *experience*.

This is ultimately what I would like your brand to become, and the reason I've written this book. You shouldn't be leading just another business in your industry. I want to help you become the BACON of your trade, sending off an irresistibly attractive sizzle that enchants potential clients and customers until they just *have* to try **you**, and after they do, they remember your brand as a delightful *experience,* and not just another replaceable product or service.

Now, insert whatever industry you're in, right on the blank below, and ask:

"So... how can I promote myself as the BACON of _____?"

I'm glad you asked! After spending almost two decades breaking down some of the most successful digital campaigns in the world, across various continents, languages, and stages of technological development, I've come upon five essential characteristics that the most successful digital marketing efforts have in common. Whereas many ineffective online efforts may have embodied one or two of these qualities, and some decent ones get to three or four, the ones that really sizzle apply **all five elements**.

The best digital efforts settle for nothing less than BACON.

You see, BACON is not just the perfect metaphor for an irresistibly attractive digital promotion, but the letters B-A-C-O-N form the acronym for the five essential qualities of outstanding digital efforts. This is what I call **the Digital BACON Formula**. The best digital efforts are:

> **Based on reality.** They throw out the wishes and whims. Great digital marketing is built on researched facts about the market and other current situations.

> **Aimed towards results.** Effective online efforts are based on measurable goals. Every initiative is informed by a plan customized to its business's needs.

> **Creatively developed.** Cookie-cutter doesn't cut it anymore. In order to stand out from the crowd, they manage to be unique and exquisitely produced.

> **Organized in propagation.** The reason they are found by their market is because they distribute their offer correctly.

> **Numerically measured.** They never measure results in the form of vague adjectives, but rather as numbers. They rely on objective measurements to know whether their efforts are moving their business forward or not.

Now, imagine what would happen to your business's marketing efforts if, instead of spending your budget on random initiatives, you strived to achieve **all five** qualities in the Digital BACON Formula!

In this book, you will learn what each of these qualities is about, as well as my process to achieve them. This book is *not* a conceptual, theoretical, philosophical journal, because I am not a "conceptual, theoretical, marketing philosopher." For many years, I've worked in the trenches with my own hands, implementing these five elements into my client's brands, while observing the record-breaking level of success it has brought them. I've also made sure my own businesses' online presences embody these qualities with tremendous results.

Now, it's *your* turn to make your online presence irresistibly attractive. Just like BACON.

Digital BACON.

CHAPTER I

The Digital BACON Process

The five aforementioned qualities in our Digital BACON Formula do not come about on their own. In order to achieve each quality, we will need a process that takes us there. Our process is comprised of five phases, each one securing a particular quality in our formula. The Digital BACON Formula is achieved by following the Digital BACON Process.

Before we look at how our Digital BACON Process works, let's look at an example of a digital effort using a different, and very common process:

Company ABC knows that it needs an online presence. Why? Because it's just what you do, right? So Company ABC goes out and hires a Web designer (after reviewing their portfolio and making sure their work looks nice, of course), and gets quoted about $3,000 for the Web design work. They consider it a fair price, and therefore go forward with it.

Along the process, the company execs tell the Web designer exactly what to do. After all, *they* know their market better than anyone else. The Web designer complies and delivers what they requested, so they're happy; that is, until they bump into some issues they simply couldn't foresee:

1) They quickly realize the $3,000 they paid for the website is not producing any measure of trackable returns. Therefore, the designer's invoice is a *cost* to them, not an investment by any stretch of the imagination.

2) They're left unclear on whether their brand is being portrayed in the proper manner online, given that they never performed research on who their competition was, nor how their brand could rise among many different other options in their industry.

3) Given that there was no strategy behind the development, there is no way to correct their course and turn their cost into a true marketing effort. Their only option is to trash the efforts up to that point, and begin the whole process from scratch.

Beginning a digital effort at the Production phase is a lot like building a commercial real estate development beginning at the construction phase. There is no analysis on where the most commercially viable spots in town are, and no blueprint to figure out what the proper structure for the building should be.

"Call in the workers, pick any spot in town, let's just start laying some bricks!"

As ridiculous as that may sound, this is unfortunately the course many businesses take when developing their online presence. Just as in the example above, there are often two very important phases that are skipped over, that must occur before the Production process even begins:

1) Discovery (to continue the analogy, the site survey)

2) Strategy (the building's blueprint in our analogy)

Only after we have an idea on what our digital landscape even looks like, and after we have determined *what* we want to accomplish, only then does it make sense to proceed towards building it, giving us:

3) Production (actually building everything according to plan)

Because of how objective the first two phases are, we will later be able to refer back to their outcome to measure whether our plan was accurate or not, and make any necessary corrections. This is what we call the Analysis phase, and it's the fifth phase in our process.

5) Analysis

In this quick summary, we've skipped over the fourth phase, so what is it? Many digital efforts, after they have gone through the Production phase, simply flip the switch and go live. The most they might do is post on social media "Hey, look at my new website," which might garner a handful of visits.

However, in this age of various and unexpected streams of information, just going live with a new website will simply not do. Launches, promotions, and even redesigns should be performed within an organized propagation plan. The world we experience around us is perceived in *phases*. When too much information comes to us out of the blue, it is usually jarring and undesirable. The same exact situation occurs in digital experiences.

Furthermore, there are some real technical concerns with regard to launching assets without proper planning. Is the web experience properly set up to track metrics? Which channels will be utilized? Under which framework will we release the different campaign assets? Launching without even thinking about these issues, let alone addressing them fully, could be irreversibly destructive.

For these reasons, we've included a fourth phase in our process:

4) Distribution

Here are the five elements of our Digital BACON Formula once again, along with each of the five corresponding phases of our Digital BACON Process:

1) Based on Reality — Discovery Phase: Analyze the current situation, both on already-released assets as well as current market considerations.

2) Aimed Towards Results — Strategy Phase: Based on information from the previous phase, determine measurable goals to achieve, plus the exact steps needed to meet those goals.

3) Creatively Developed — Production Phase: Execute all the assets required to run the strategy, in a unique and creatively exquisite manner.

4) Organized in Propagation — Distribution Phase: Output the assets executed in the previous phase, according to an organized plan.

5) Numerically Measured — Analysis Phase: Measure the success or failure of all previous steps, and determining correction and/or optimization opportunities.

As you can see, each phase after the first feeds from the information laid out in the one previous to it. Most problems with ineffective digital efforts will invariably occur because one phase kicked off without being properly informed — and this usually happens because there was no prior phase in place at all!

These phases are also cyclical. For example, issues or opportunities identified in the Analysis phase will reveal details to be addressed in any of the prior four phases. Maybe new research needs to be considered, so going back to the Discovery phase is required. Or maybe some assets need to be optimized for better conversion opportunities, so we return to the Production phase to address this.

The Digital BACON Process helps ensure that your digital investment is well planned, that objectives are set, and that each phase works towards meeting those objectives.

The purpose of this book is not to give you the exact strategy you must follow, nor the goals you must meet. That is for your company to decide (you may consider contacting a digital marketing agency for further help — more info about that at the end of the book). The idea here is to lay out the ideal *process* to help you reach the five essential qualities in the Digital BACON Formula.

In the following chapters, we will go in-depth into

each of these phases, and will describe effective methods to help you deploy an irresistibly attractive online presence for your brand.

Ready? Let's go!

CHAPTER II

Based On Reality

DISCOVERY PHASE

My family and I enjoy going out every year — sometimes even twice a year — on a camping trip. We enjoy being in the outdoors, relaxing and calling that little space in the wilderness *ours,* if only for a few days.

When planning our camping trips, there are many different elements to consider. Do we want to go in the fall or winter, when the weather will be much colder? Or would we rather go in the spring or summer? Maybe camp near the sea or by a river? Are there certain amenities that interest us, such as a playground, sports activities, or a beach? At the end of the day, we need to consider these options within what is available at the time we begin booking our trip.

On one of our trips, which occurred during the summer, a friend of ours invited us to a certain campsite. He told us there was a river nearby, where one could jump in and float downstream for about three hours until you reached the other end. Once the river trip ended, you could take a shuttle bus back to the camp site. He told us the river had one of the clearest waters in the whole United States, a scientifically proven fact! It really sounded like a lot of fun!

We needed no more convincing, so we booked the first campsite that became available. We were so excited about the amenities, that of course, we forgot to research other important factors.

When we got there, we encountered the first issue: the campsite we reserved was in a very open area, with no trees surrounding it. This meant that the hot sun was going to hit our tents directly. To  make matters worse, the ground at that particular campsite was not earth — as commonly found at most other campsites — but gravel with bedrock underneath. The sun wouldn't only hit us from above, but also heat the rocks and fry us from below! Also, the ground was so hard that our standard tent spikes couldn't pierce through it, so we had to drive out to a hardware store to buy huge tent spikes — they looked to me like old-fashioned railroad nails — and a carpenter's hammer, as our puny rubber mallet just wouldn't do.

Sure enough, we enjoyed the river, but the camping experience itself was miserable! With the proper research, we would have been better prepared, or could have avoided the issues completely.

This short story is very similar to what happens to businesses that set up their digital presence without the proper research on *reality*. They get so excited about showing their product or service, that they end up taking a very poor effort live, one which was only aligned to their desires and personal tastes. They forget about "surveying the landscape," so to speak, and are then trapped with time and money invested into an effort that simply does not produce any results.

Furthermore, in order for your offer to be *irresistibly attractive*, it is absolutely essential that you have knowledge on what your audience is *currently* attracted to, and what other options are currently satisfying their need in some measure or another.

Let's discuss what a proper Discovery phase entails, as well as some ideas on how to accomplish each step.

> You can download my Discovery Worksheet
> for free from this link:
> www.cstps.co/DiscoveryWorksheet

Feel free to print it, and as you read the description for each Discovery step, fill each section in with your thoughts and findings. Reading through this book is great to give you a general idea of what we're going for, but taking action at each step will actually get you ready for the next phase.

YOUR CURRENT SITUATION

Does your company currently have a Web presence? If not, you can just skip over to the next sub-segment, "Product/Service Description." If you've already deployed a digital marketing effort, and are reading this book in order to learn how to optimize it, keep reading.

Taking a deep snapshot of your current Web efforts is absolutely necessary to understand what we're moving forward from. This step will demand a level of honesty and patience to assess details you may have proceeded forward without possession of the proper knowledge.

When I said *"deep snapshot,"* did you think about screen captures of your website? Those might be good to archive, but what we're looking for is much more. We want to retrieve data and analytics that describe the current situation as much as possible.

The following are the essentials we need to find out.

SITE DISCOVERY

PageRank: This is the level of authority a domain name has in Google's eyes. The higher the PageRank, the more trustworthy its pages are — and in most cases, its outgoing links as well. Just search "check pagerank" in Google, and choose one of the many tools available in the results. Any of those tools will ask for your URL (website address). Once the result comes up, take a note of your PageRank score.

Alexa Rank: www.cstps.co/alexa tallies the popularity of different web properties across the web, along with a few other metrics. Don't be too overwhelmed by the results for now. Just make note of your web properties' ranking.

Backlinks: These are links to your site from other sites, which tell the search engines that yours is a site to pay attention to. There a few sites to do this, but my favorite right now is www.cstps.co/majestic. Search up your site's URL, and write down the results for External Backlinks, Trust Flow, and Citation Flow.

Average Visits per Month: If you or your web developer remembered to install a tracking system (I certainly hope so!), pull up your report. Take a sampling of different months during the year, and average the amount of visits per month your site has received. Write this number down.

Popular Content: If you have a metrics report as described previously, you should be able to determine if you have content that is above and beyond the rest in popularity. If it's still receiving a steady flow of organic traffic, you might want to preserve its URL. Make a list of your top content, along with their URLs.

Organic Traffic: If you use Google Analytics for tracking, not so long ago they encrypted organic traffic results, and because of this, you cannot see these under the dashboard as before. However, if you or your web developer remembered to register your domain under Google Webmaster Tools, you will still be able to pull up *some* data. Go to Search Traffic, and then Search Queries to find a list of organic terms pointing to your site. It is useful to know which search terms turn up with your site in the results, especially if they make first page. Make special note of any results scoring a "1" under the "Avg Position" column.

Referral Sites: If you can go back to Google Analytics, visit the section under Acquisition/All referrals. Write down the top 10 sites currently or recently sending you traffic.

Conversion rate: If your site depends on conversions (as it should be in most cases), do you have data on how many visitors are converting? If you have an average number of your conversions per month, multiply that number by 100, and then divide that result by the average number of visitors per month. Stated as a percentage, this is your average conversion rate.

SOCIAL MEDIA DISCOVERY

Many people get caught up on the "numbers game" of followers, friends, and likes on social media. This is really not *that* important to us, but it's good to make note of the current situation. No matter if it's Facebook, Twitter, or Snapinstavinegram *(okay, I just made that last one up)*, you'll want to fill in the chart with the metrics for each channel, like this:

Name of social network	
Date profile was created	
Number of text posts loaded	
Number of photos loaded	
Number of followers	
Engagement (high, medium, low)	
Notes on Paid Traffic:	
Best traffic referrer? (YES/NO)	

In the last column, you're going to want to make note if a particular social network has been responsible for a high amount of visits to your digital properties, which may signal a good amount of link engagement/conversion.

For the next-to-last column, you definitely want to add a note if there have been paid advertising efforts in the past. Which methods were used exactly? Were those successful? Why or why not? Any insights that can be gleaned from this will be valuable for our Strategy and Distribution phases.

PRESS DISCOVERY

Which media entities — either online and offline — have made mention of your company and/or web address? Whether it's been positive or negative, you're going to want to jot this list down, as well as the titles of the relevant articles, and where they can be found.

If your brand has a ton of user reviews, it may not be as important to log all of them. My agency collects thousands of user reviews and organizes the data in easy-to-read graphs to determine overarching tendencies, but this is an intense process and you may not have the time nor resources for it. Pull up a few representative samples of good and bad reviews, and if necessary, summarize the insights you can learn from each of those.

The information you've collected so far should be enough to store as your "Current Situation Snapshot". Let's move on towards issues about the brand itself.

WHAT DO YOU REALLY OFFER?

In the first space, fill in the name of your product/ service. Then right below it, write one or two sentences describing what it is that you offer to your potential clients and customers.

Now, a proper Discovery should begin with understanding, in as clear a manner as possible, what it is that you are trying to sell (or communicate). Yes, I know this sounds ridiculous. If you picked up this book, *of course* you know what you're selling. You just filled it in while reading the previous paragraph!

However, I will risk insulting you by questioning your assumption.

Many of us are so engrossed into our respective businesses, that we forget a key fact. **What we *think* we sell is irrelevant.** The way you dreamed up your product/service, the years you put into it, the passion you have for it, the amazing team behind it, it's all irrelevant if your offer doesn't satisfy a functional need for someone else.

Let's begin by identifying the top three *real* problems your audience has that you are looking to solve. For example, if your company offers financial advice, one of the problems could be that customers need assistance on how to best invest their money for a great return in the future. Or if your company provides office cleaning services, the real problem could be that businesses need to have a tidy space, as anything less could affect the perception from their clients and therefore affect sales. Spend some time thinking about three *real* problems (emphasis on "real"), and write these down.

See those problems? Whatever your product/service is, it will only be relevant as long as it addresses these issues. You could have dreamed up a perfect accounting practice while lying on a hammock with a piña colada in your left hand and a perfect circle of seagulls fluttering around, which is why your logo has a picture of a seagull taking a bath inside of a piña colada, but if you can't help me organize my books to reduce my tax liability — a possible *real* problem for a customer, I will care very little about the crazy stories or your... "creative" brand choices.

Now ask yourself: What are the three solutions that *directly* address the top three problems we've already identified? Write these down on the list at the right.

After you've done this, rewrite your product/service description by incorporating the three solutions you just wrote down. In other words, make the three into a sentence or two.

Does this description sound unique enough? If not, we may need to give it a bit more thought to give it a personalized spin. The goal is to be unique enough to stand out from the competition. (We'll do some competitive analysis a bit later, but you probably know enough to make your product/description unique.)

If this new description is not drastically different from the one you initially wrote at the top, congratulations! It looks like you were clear all along. In most cases, however, my clients end up with something quite different, or at least with some subtle yet significant differences.

PURCHASE DRIVERS

Back to the worksheet, let's write the top three purchase drivers for your offer, in order of importance, from the list below. What we're looking for are aspects that make your offer unique in the marketplace, and that communicate to the audience that your offer is simply the one to purchase. Choose from this list:

- **Price:** Is the price point appealing?
- **Quality:** Does your offer have unmatched quality?
- **Style:** Is the style unique, outstanding, and supremely attractive?
- **Emotional connection:** Does your offer appeal to the audience in a strong, emotional way?
- **Cultural connection:** Does your offer appeal to an audience's cultural identity?
- **Gender connection:** Is your offer appealing to a specific gender in a strong way?
- **Racial connection:** Is your offer meant to appeal to an audience's racial makeup?
- **Geographic identity:** Does your offer embody aspects of a certain geographic area that are very firmly attractive?
- **Philosophic connection:** Does your offer appeal to your audience's beliefs or ideology?
- **Convenience:** Does your offer make your audience's life easier in some way?

Notice that from here forward, I will not refer to your product or service any more. As I've explained, this is utterly irrelevant. Throughout the rest of the book, we will refocus our efforts on promoting **your offer**, which is the set of solutions you are putting forth to address very particular and real problems your audience is dealing with, in exchange for some type of value. Smart digital marketing doesn't promote products, services, nor brands online. We market our specific **offers**.

I've placed an article with even more tips to reshape your offer into one that is irresistibly attractive here: www.cstps.co/oia

KEYWORDS

Place yourself in your customer's shoes for a second and ask yourself: "When my customer is online, what would they type into their search engine in order to find my offer?" The words that organically come off of your customer's fingers onto their keyboards are what we call "keywords." Determining what these keywords are early in the game will be fantastic, as they will help us discover consumer patterns along the way, and will also guide us as to how we should phrase our offer.

Ideally, you'll be looking to determine 1-3 words that spell out your consumer's first thought when trying to look up what you have to offer. Some offers may require longer keywords, and that's perfectly fine. As long as we're shaving down to *exactly* the words we require, we should be in good shape.

We will also be determining a primary keyword — which will be the driving force behind our efforts — along with many secondary keywords. These keywords could be side thoughts and related topics when people think about your offer. Also, they might be the names of the different components of your offer, whether it's seasonal events, additional services, etc. Just make sure they're all *relevant* to your offer.

Relevancy is one of four main criteria we will

consider at this early stage, along with Commerciality, Volume, and Competition.

1) Relevancy: How close-knitted is the keyword to the actual subject of our offer?

For example, if our offer includes coaching for runners, it would be terribly unfocused to select "sports assistance" as our keyword. It's just too broad, as people looking for football coaching and sports psychology may also be using that term. "Runners coaching" might be the perfect keyword. As obvious as this may sound, you would be surprised at the amount of businesses that get too creative with their keywords. Remember we're not developing ad copy here. We're trying to get into our consumer's psyche, and predict what they ask the search engines when they're looking to buy what you offer.

Let's eliminate every keyword that doesn't *directly* relate to our offer, and add a few more that would direct consumers straight towards it.

2) Commerciality: How much does the keyword reveal a buyer's true intent?

Some keywords are pretty open-ended and don't really tell us whether the person searching has any intent to pull out their wallet and send you cash. You must take a step back, and think which keywords a person would use when looking on the Web for your offer.

Our previous example, "runners coaching," can be used for people looking to hire a running coach, but also by someone trying to learn how to *become* a running coach — trying to become your competition!

For each keyword you think of, a good exercise is to place it within a grid like the one below, and see if we can rewrite it and move it up the commerciality ladder.

Low/unknown Commerciality	Moderate Commerciality	High Commerciality
runners coach	find runners coach	hire runners coach

A cool little trick to help you brainstorm keyword variations is Google's auto-suggest feature:

1. Go to Google.com.
2. Start typing the main words of your offer.
3. In the dropdown, several popular word combinations will come up.
4. Repeat this process, beginning with different keywords each time.

3) Volume: How many searches occur for this keyword?

It wouldn't be helpful that we found what may seem like great keywords if nobody is actually using them to find anything on the Web. This is actually one of the primary reasons why we're doing this exercise so early in the game. We want to find out which search terms people are *actually* interested in, and judge the level of interest by the amount of searches in a determined period of time.

I use a specialized set of tools for this, but the best free one is — you guessed it — Google. Log into adwords.google.com (you may need to create a new account), and under "Tools" you'll find Google's Keyword Planner. Once there, you'll be able to copy and paste your list of keywords, and observe an estimated amount of monthly searches that have occurred for each one. Now, Google's numbers are unfortunately not precise, so you need to play it by ear from here. In spite of this, the numbers do point towards which keywords are searched more than others, relatively speaking.

At this point, you may want to set aside keywords that have little to no search volume, as they're probably not worth focusing on as your primary keyword.

4) Competition: How many other web properties are already fighting for this keyword?

Competition for keywords may make us shy away, but high competition is usually the X that marks the spot where treasure can be dug up, although it usually also shows us where it will be most difficult to introduce our offer.

While Google's Keyword Tool also shows a column for "Competition," I've found that this is not very reliable. The best free alternative is staring you right in the face: Just take the plunge and go through the search experience as a user.

Input your keyword into the search field on Google, and then look at the results page. Then answer "yes" or "no" to the following three questions:

1. Do you see large global brands dominating the first 3-5 results? **YES   NO**

2. Are there lots of ads above and to the side of the search results? **YES   NO**

3. Are there irrelevant or confusing results in the first 3-5 results? **YES   NO**

If you answered YES to the first two questions, your keyword has loads of competition. However, if you answered NO to the first two, and YES to the last question, you may have found a keyword with low competition that could be much easier to rank for.

Remember to judge your primary keyword under all four criteria! Low competition should be only one factor to judge by.

Within these four criteria, the sweet spot you should strive for when looking for a primary keyword looks like this:

Relevancy: HIGH	Commerciality: HIGH
Volume: HIGH	Competition: LOW

If your keyword has these four qualities as described above, you may have found a true gold mine! If it only scores on two or three of the four, at least make sure Relevancy is one of those, and that the others are as close as possible to the benchmark we've described above.

Now would be a good time to write down the primary keyword and secondary keywords you have in mind for your offer — your bookmark (or index finger) will be right here saving your place when you're done.

COMPETITIVE ANALYSIS

Once we've clarified our offer, we need to be aware of how much competition for the same or similar offers already exists online. The three reasons for this are:

Market potential cannot be measured on its own if we're not taking into consideration the amount of competition we will face. We simply cannot value the potential for business based on demand alone, but also by understanding who is currently supplying that demand.

The level of competition **must** inform our strategy later on. A digital marketing plan for a niche with low competition will be entirely different from one where other players are aggressively investing in dominating the market.

In many cases, we can glean fantastic insight from what the competition has already done — whether it's on what to do to be successful (we can assume they're already investing good money doing things right), what not to do, or which things to do better than them.

We will address point two later on in our chapter on the Strategy step. For now, let me show you what we can do about points one and three.

Based on your offer's description and keyword research, you'll have a pretty good idea of how your audience begins looking for what you have to offer. If the great majority of your market types in the URLs of your competitors directly, there's really not much you can do, other than hack their websites *(...I didn't just type that, did I?... Bad Alex... bad, bad Alex...).*

However, if your potential audience searches the web freely — and in most cases, they do — we can assume that we can find out how much of the digital market is taken over, and whether there is any space left for us to crawl in.

Google's Keyword Tool has a "Competition" column in its results, but as I mentioned, it's not very accurate. Also, their "Low," "Medium," and "High" marks really don't communicate much to me, in terms of *exactly how* a result is competitive under those criteria.

I favor an entirely different method. The first thing we need to do is to navigate the web as if we were our own intended audience. Which search engines do they go to first? What search terms do they use? This would be your best testing ground at this point.

Tip: An even better method would be to find someone else — preferably someone within your target audience — to search for your offer, who hasn't read your offer description. What comes to mind first when they begin their search?

Take a look at a few of the search engine results pages. What do you see?

For each search term, mark a check on its corresponding box:

Is the page filled (top and/or side) with advertising from other competitors?

Are the top 3-5 results dominated by large brand names?

Are the top 3-5 results not brand names, but highly relevant articles or posts?

Are the top 3-5 results high PageRank domains?*
See my short explanation on PageRank under "Site Discovery" on page 28.

If you checked even one of these boxes, you can count on that search term being highly competitive. No need to get discouraged quite yet, though.

If there are brand names that continually come up alongside your offer, you're going to want to make note of the top 5-8. Once you have this list, check out the ad copy they use to drive visitors to their site. We're not looking to copy them, only to gain information on the type of words they've decided to work with. Naturally, we won't have any data on whether the ad copy is working for them, so there's no need to get too hung up on this. What we want to do is at least observe if there are any patterns we can discern on what they often choose to do.

You may find this exercise interesting for another reason. If you're looking to carve out a niche in the marketplace, by analyzing where your competitors are all playing, you may find out where they're *not* playing. Are there any terms or market segments you think are being forgotten or overlooked by them? If so, make note of this.

One little trick — as imprecise as it may be, it's still helpful — is to go into Facebook's Ad Manager , which can be found at www.cstps.co/facebookads. Begin creating a new ad (don't worry, we won't actually deploy the ad), and under the criteria of "Interests," input the name of your competitor's brand. Once you do this, look on the right side under "Potential Reach." This will give you an approximate idea of the number of people on Facebook who have cited that brand as one of their favorites. Feel free to measure sub-segments of that reach, such as geography, gender, etc. It's generally not a good idea to choose too many criteria at once, as we don't want to segment too much. Go through these one by one.

One last trick is to take the URL of your top 8-10 competitors, place it in quotes, and run a Google search for it. Then look at where it says "About xxx,xxx results." Also run the exact same search for the competitor's brand name spelled out.

As you dig up these findings, fill in a grid similar to this one:

Competition	ABC
Uses paid ads?	YES
Is in the top results on search engines?	YES
Has a high PR domain?	YES
Has a massive (>1 million) group of fans on Facebook?	YES
Has more than 100,000 sites mentioning its URL?	YES
Has more than 1 million sites mentioning its brand name?	YES

If you fill in a chart like this — with YES on each space — for any of your competitors, it's the definition of going up against an 800-pound gorilla, and you will probably need to be very creative with your strategy. We dedicate a whole chapter on Strategy discussion alone, so don't worry too much about it for now.

The last thing you should do for each of the competitors you have been able to identify is research what they are offering. Find out if it either partially or fully also solves your target audience's problem. Right beside each offer include the price they demand in exchange for said solution.

Now, fill in the Competitive Analysis section of our Discovery Worksheet with the information you now know. I've placed more detailed instructions on how to fill in each section here: www.cstps.co/competitiveanalysis

THE "SWOT" SNAPSHOT

Everything we've described up to this point should be giving you a pretty clear idea of what your current online situation is. Now it's time to create what we'll call a SWOT Snapshot, which will describe our current situation in four very distinct aspects: Strengths, Weaknesses, Opportunities, and Threats. Each is described below.

After you read each description, go to your Discovery Worksheet and fill out three sentences under each quadrant. You may find you want to limit yourself to just one or two, but if you aim for three, you'll push yourself to find more insights and resist the urge to brush off something that is crying for attention.

STRENGTHS

Up to this point, you will have surely discovered many wonderful things your brand or business has done correctly in the digital space up to this point, or some awesome achievements that you've reached. Feel free to boast, but also let's keep things as down to earth as possible. Don't include anything that didn't come as a direct result of intentional digital decisions, or that is not repeatable. Winning the lottery is not a strength, but recognizing opportunities and profiting from them definitely are.

A few ideas that might kick start your strengths list:

"We exceeded sales expectations last ..."

"We have a customer database of ..."

"Our product has been reviewed by ..."

"We come up first on the search results for ..."

Feel free to add anything else that you consider makes your offer strong.

WEAKNESSES

Just as you've listed the great things your brand can claim for itself, it's time to get honest about the not-so-great issues that haunt you time after time. Again, don't write down accidental issues, unless they're the direct result of poor decisions or operations.

Some examples could be:

"Our server's downtime has affected sales several times ..."

"Our product is not being found under the most relevant search terms ..."

"Too much time passes between our product launches and when we see sales come in ..."

"Our conversion rate is very low ..."

OPPORTUNITIES

Now let's think of a question: If we continue supporting our strengths, and/or improve our offer in new ways, what would that do for our online presence? Think about breakthroughs that are within our reach, but also some that are idealistic (without exaggerating, though). Starting each statement with the word "if" is a good practice, as this will keep us thinking about what will directly cause a breakthrough in opportunity.

A few ideas to get you started:

"If we sustain and grow our customer database, we'll have a fantastic launch ..."

"If we increase our ranking for our primary keyword, we'll ..."

"If we optimize our web presence, we can increase..."

"If we stick to our content strategy, we'll have ..."

THREATS

While the previous step described optimistic possibilities, in this one we'll allow ourselves to be a bit pessimistic. What would happen if we didn't sustain our strengths, or if we didn't correct our weaknesses? We want to be as descriptive as possible, but without going into a doom-and-gloom party. Again, beginning each statement with the word "if" is a great way to keep our thoughts within causes and consequences. Examples:

"If we lose our standing in search engines, our competition will ..."

"If we don't fix our server situation, we will ..."

"If we don't pick up our conversion rate, our sales for this year will ..."

"If we can't increase our customer satisfaction rate, we ..."

Once again, add three statements under each quadrant in the following chart:

Strengths	Weaknesses
1. 2. 3.	1. 2. 3.
Opportunities 1. 2. 3.	**Threats** 1. 2. 3.

AUDIENCE PROFILE

One of the aspects that we absolutely must clarify in order to compose our offer is figuring out who our ideal audience is. The two criteria to determine your primary target audience can be defined very simply:

1) Who is most likely to buy into your offer?

2) How profitable is this audience?

Many companies tend to over-simplify this very important detail. They will move forward with a one-dimensional description, such as "women" or "people older than 50." In order to ensure our Strategy is as successful as can be, we're going to need to get much more detailed than this.

What if your business sells to other businesses? Many of the criteria will apply to determining how to reach the ideal businesses that will buy what you sell. Alternatively, you can focus on the decision-makers in those businesses, and create an audience profile around them. At the end of the day, you will want to present a compelling offer that at least one person will make a decision to purchase or pass on. Who is this person? The exercises here will help you figure this out.

The minimum criteria we recommend you carefully examine are:

Geography: Where does your ideal audience live?

Seasonal considerations: When are they most likely looking for your services?

Demographics: What is their age, race, cultural background, gender, marital status, family composition, and other details that describe them?

Preferences/Lifestyle: What are their likes/dislikes?

Let's go in detail on each of these. I'll also go into some of my favorite techniques to figure out insights on each of these very quickly.

GEOGRAPHY

It's a fact that we live in a connected world. Particularly in the field of digital marketing, we know that our message can be projected throughout the world very easily. However, focusing on the whole planet amounts to not focusing at all. In order to make the best use of our resources, we need to hone in on which areas are more likely to buy what we offer.

Of course, the answer to this question can be as large as a continent, or as small as a town. Yet just identifying one of these is a huge success, versus  just throwing darts in the darkness, or choosing the city you live in just because that's where you are. Besides, why would you ever stick with just your own city? Unless your offer only applies to local clients, of course. In that case, you already have your geographic profile pretty much figured out!

If you already have a sales history, it might be pretty easy for you to dig that up, and find out where the majority of your sales have come from. However, even in this case, you may want to explore additional markets that you haven't considered up to this point.

One of my favorite tools to explore interest in a particular brand or topic is Google Trends (www.cstps.co/googletrends).

Google Trends is an ideal tool for figuring out which areas are showing the most interest in your offer, down to the region, state, and even city level. Also, the information on Google Trends is constantly being updated. Additionally, it includes historical data as well.

For example, if your offer includes financial advice, as of the date I'm writing this book, the top five countries seeking for this service are:

United States
United Kingdom
Canada
Australia
Ireland

You may have already decided that it's more convenient for you to work with clients in the United States, so at this point that information isn't groundbreaking, as it aligns with your business operations. However, if you click on "United States," you get another top five list by state, which today looks like this:

New Jersey
New York
Minnesota
Pennsylvania
Massachusetts

Amazing, right? Now let's click on "Minnesota" to see a new list:

Minneapolis
Hopkins
Saint Paul
Saint Cloud

If we were able to pull up four results for each of those top five states, we immediately end up with the top twenty cities in the United States looking for your offer. Think about what you could do with that knowledge!

Again, this is not related to top areas *already offering* your services, but rather areas where there are the most searches for what you're selling.

Instead of throwing darts all over the world, with this knowledge you can focus your strategy precisely on where it will most likely have the effect you desire ... buying from you!

A great exercise is to repeat the process I just outlined, but with related/secondary topics. In the case of "financial advice," what are some of the specific services you offer? Retirement plans? Investment advice? Just run a similar search for each of these, and you may garner some more juicy insights you may not have been considering.

TIP: Some of the search terms might result in a message such as, "there is not enough search volume to show results." If so, you might need to go a bit broader with your search term. For example, instead of saying "neckties for men" start with "men's apparel," then dig one step deeper from there.

SEASONAL CONSIDERATIONS

Your offer may be evergreen, in the sense that there is a demand for it all year long, or it may be seasonal, or somewhere in between. Either way, this is essential to keep in mind as well. It would make no sense to spend the same amount of your resources all year long, when most of the demand happens at a certain period of the year.

Here are some examples of clearly evergreen offers, and others that are clearly seasonal:

Evergreen	Seasonal
Toilet paper	Christmas ornaments
Books	Chocolate Easter bunnies
Shoes	Home winterizing services
Water bottles	Beach balls
Birthday cards	Mother's Day cards

Even after understanding this framework, there might be demand for seasonal items at other times of the year (I know of people looking for Christmas ornaments in July!), and the demand for the evergreen offers may increase or decrease slightly throughout the year. In any case, the offers in the right column peak drastically at a certain point in the year, whereas the examples on the left are mostly the same throughout the year.

You might already be aware that your offer has certain peaks throughout the year, but may be surprised at when exactly they occur.

Let's say you sell equipment for baseball players. Someone like me, who doesn't have a clue when baseball seasons begin and end, can find out very quickly when the market-demand seasons happen, which is really all that matters to a non-baseball fan marketer like me!

Pull up Google Trends, and input the keyword "baseball gear." We can immediately notice two things. First, there is a clear peak of interest beginning in March that begins to slope down (but not as a sudden drop either) right around April. Secondly,

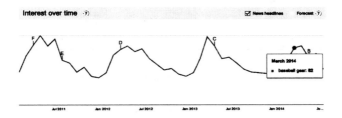

this timely peak has been a pretty predictable pattern for the last 10 years, which is as far back as the data shows — it could be more.

Be aware of the patterns of your market, and take them into account within your digital marketing strategy.

DEMOGRAPHICS

You might want to think that your offer is so great that every single individual on the planet is a candidate to hand you money, but let's be real: there is most likely a certain range of consumers that will be interested in it. It's not that anyone *couldn't* buy. What we're looking to determine is purchase likelihood. If we market to our more likely buyer, we'll be cutting through to the largest segment of our market first, thus ensuring a greater volume of sales.

Many businesses already have enough data to determine the type of individual who has purchased from them the most in the past. In that case, this exercise will be mostly internal, performed by wrangling that data and analyzing it to determine the trends.

However, even in these cases, it may be a worthwhile exercise to question these findings, and seek out whether there are other markets that may have been overlooked.

A few guidelines when determining your offer's demographics:

Remember to keep things honest and commercially viable. In simple terms, *keep it real*. We're trying to determine who is *likely* to buy, not who *you* would enjoy selling to. Unless those align, keep it weighted towards the first criteria: who is most likely to buy what you're offering?

Depending on your offer, it may not be a good idea to go too narrow, so as not to close ourselves to the market too much; however, the opposite is true as well. Making our criteria too wide defeats the purpose of defining a market at all. Always question whether we're closing or widening our reach unnecessarily.

The typical criteria for demographic profiling are:

- **Age:** Several classifications are possible, whether by ranges (e.g., 25-35 years old) or by generational labels (e.g., Baby Boomers, Generation X, etc.), birth year ranges, or some other method.
- **Gender:** Whether the simple male/female binary classification model, or any of the more recent sub-classifications. There are just too many to count, and the list seems to keep growing!
- **Marital Status:** Married, single, and other sub-variants.

- **Household income:** A rough idea of how much spending power exists in the person's house.
- **Employment status:** Employed, unemployed, self-employed, etc.
- **Industry of employment:** Which field your target consumer works in.
- **Education:** High school, college, etc.
- **Ethnicity/Race:** If relevant to your offer.
- **Parental Status:** Has children at home, has children living elsewhere, wants children, etc.
- **Number of Children:** In precise numbers or in ranges.

PSYCHOGRAPHICS

Though it may sound like the place where Alfred Hitchcock got his business cards, Psychographics just refer to the psychological profile that defines our target individual.

Depending on what your offer is, you may want to consider using a Psychographics profile instead of a Demographics profile, although it's perfectly fine — and will make your audience profile stronger — if you decide to use both models.

A relevant Psychographic profile will be one that is not too far removed from the essence of your offer. In other words, the components involved will not be unrelated to your offer, so as to avoid closing up the target market too much.

Typical Psychographic criteria are:

- **Preferred Activities:** What does your target individual occupy their time with? You can include outdoor situations, as well as activities within their homes.

- **Interests:** What are the topics your target is interested in? We can also ask this in a less abstract way: What publications, TV shows, websites, etc., does your target tend to read and view?
- **Opinions:** If your offer requires a certain stand on an issue or subject, you should make note of it here.
- **Attitudes:** What is your target's outlook on life? How do they respond to certain stimuli?
- **Values:** What is their ethical stance, and what is it based on?
- **Behaviors:** Are there any recognizable and particular patterns in what they do, above baseline actions needed for survival?

Fill in the Audience Profile section of your Discovery Worksheet with the insights you've arrived at up to this point.

FOCUS GROUPS / SURVEYS

If you feel like you still don't know enough about your audience, or just want to go a different route, you can always conduct a focus group or survey to help you refine your target market, and inform you about a segment you've been considering. Naturally, you can hire a specialized agency to help you coordinate any of these at a massive scale, though in some cases this can be quite expensive.

There are, however, some bootstrapped ways to go about learning more about your audience. Think about people you already know who might be in the ideal target market for your offer. You might be surprised at how many of them are in your address book or social media channels, or how many of your contacts could refer you to people you might be able to reach out to.

Surveys. I once needed a particular behavioral profile for a project I was working on, so I went to Google Forms and typed in my questions. Then I shared the link to the form on all my social media accounts, and asked my contacts to please share it with any people within my target audience that they knew. I did not use paid advertisements, nor did I offer any incentives. What I got in return were *85 responses*, and saved more than $3,000 in the process.

It's amazing what your friends and contacts will do to help you. Naturally, you don't ever want to abuse their kindness. If you have resorted to them too many times in a short period of time, you may need to consider paid traffic and/or an incentive. However, these routes may still be more inexpensive than hiring a research agency.

Focus Groups. You also can arrange a live session at your office with different people of a certain segment. Ask them specific questions, and write each response down. Better yet, shoot video of the whole session so you can review the reactions later.

Be careful about assuming too much from just a small number of people chatting it up about a subject. When you're looking for trends, the more people you research, the better.

SOCIAL LISTENING

With the amazing amount of quality data that can be found on social media, some agencies like mine have been offering social listening technology to businesses. You can now "eavesdrop" into opinions and dialogues about your subject matter, compile those data, and discover fundamentally important trends for your business.

You might be able to grab a small sampling of conversations from places where people are talking about your subject of industry, which will give you great insight into how that audience thinks and acts.

A few places you may want to research:

Social channels: Look for keywords that represent words or phrases that people normally use when talking about your subject matter. You might encounter your own competition peddling their goods, but you'll also find some good insights. Do this on:

Twitter: search.twitter.com

Google+: Log into plus.google.com, use the search box at the top.

Facebook: The search function in Facebook is not as useful as the other ones, but you still might be able to pull in a few useful posts.

Forums: There are a ton of online forums, where your audience is mingling right now. To find which they are, go to Google, and search for your industry topic + the word "forum."

Reviews: Some industries have independent sites that let users review their product or service.

Don't fall into the temptation of interacting with these folks. All we're doing is listening to what they're saying, and taking note of any important insights that will inform our Audience Profile even further.

CREATING A PERSONA

The word "Persona" is Latin in origin, and referred to a mask that an actor would wear during a theatrical presentation. In the same manner, a *Persona* in marketing refers to a fictitious individual's identity that we "carve out," based on the audience profile we've just identified.

A persona should be as specifically defined as possible, if we want it to be useful for our purposes. Think about your persona as a character in your story; the story of your market. This character will be used for you to look through as a mask, and constantly question how this character would view your offer and how it is presented.

The good news is, if you've been following along step-by-step up to this point, you already have all the elements needed to build your persona. If you haven't been filling out each step of the way, I strongly recommend you go back to page 47 and do so. It's going to be a lot more difficult to build a persona without thinking about each individual component of your Audience Profile — besides, it will be mere guesswork and not really useful.

HOW TO BUILD A PERFECT PERSONA

For each of the criteria you've drawn up, you will choose one quality that is within the ranges or is exactly the same as you've specified. In the case of ranges, a good idea is to find a quality within the average range, and preferably not toward either extreme.

Come up with a characteristic that is representative of your character's gender, marital status, geography, age, parental status, ethnicity/race (if relevant), and number of children, give him/her a name, and combine them all in one sentence. For example: "Martha is a 29-year-old Hispanic woman, who lives in Hoboken, New Jersey, with her husband and two children."

Your second sentence will describe her occupation and activities, as you've drawn up previously. For example: "She is a manager at a local hardware store where she earns $60,000 per year, and on the weekends enjoys spending time outdoors with her family."

Your third sentence will outline some of her values, opinions, attitudes, and behaviors. There's no need to get too descriptive for each of these, only as far as characteristics that would stand out. For example: "Martha is very concerned about social justice and conservative family values. She tends to watch TV networks like CNN and Telemundo, and enjoys reading *Home and Garden Magazine*."

Your fourth sentence in the persona is going to describe a bit more detail from any of the previous criteria that you see directly related to your offer. In other words, what aspect of their life makes them see value in what you offer? For this, you can also refer back to your notes when describing your audience's top three real problems. For example, if your offer is pet grooming, it could look something like this: "She loves her two dogs, but often struggles finding the time and energy to keep them well-groomed."

After you've drawn up your four sentences, you can go back and fill in some more details about your persona. Expand on any of the sections as you see fit, but only if you feel you need further description to bring your persona to life.

Bonus Tip: Want to take your persona from perfect to *incredibly perfect*? After you have a strong persona description, go to images.google.com, and input a few keywords that describe him/her, along with the word "headshot" (for our example above, you could use the terms *"Hispanic mom headshot"*). Look over the images that come up, and choose the one that best represents your persona. Right-click it in your browser and select the option to save the image to your hard drive. (IMPORTANT: We are only using this image for internal and referential use, **not** for our advertisements nor designs. It's very important to respect the original owner's rights of public usage.)

BONUS Bonus Tip: If we really want to bring our incredibly perfect persona to life, add a few quotes he/she would say about the subject matter directly related to your offer, and in line with the exploration we just performed. For example, "I love my dogs, but it's a hassle to groom them during the only time I have to relax!" One to three quotes like this will really help you see your target audience's needs from a real, human viewpoint. There's nothing that creates insights into another person's mind than their words, and even though this is mere — although substantiated — fabrication, as you write it, you will notice if they're natural or too contrived.

Now, place the photo on a page, paste the quotes beside it, and then add the bio of our persona below. Refer to this persona throughout the next phase, and even print and paste it on your wall if you feel it helps you keep it top of mind.

TEN BIG LESSONS

Our final step in our Discovery phase is to refer back to everything we've dug up during our exploration, and write down the 10 items that stand out the most from your worksheet at this point. Did anything capture our attention in a special way? Maybe some insight surprised us? Did a particular way of looking at our offer seem fresh and unique?

These are things we will want to write down as our Ten Big Lessons on our Discovery worksheet. Again, you can download it for free here: www.cstps.co/DiscoveryWorksheet)

Why 10 items? What I've found is that when most businesses work on their digital strategy, they only keep 1-2 topics in mind. Usually, it's treated as a "point A to point B" exercise, but the reality is that a well-thought strategy should involve many more insights than this. Expanding this common standard further will force us to think deeply, and consider our offer and our goals from a big-picture, multi-dimensional standpoint.

Once you've written down your Ten Big Lessons, collect all the worksheets you've filled in up to this point, and move on to the next phase: *Strategy*.

"To win by strategy is no less the role of a

general than to win by arms."

— Julius Caesar

CHAPTER III

Aimed Towards Results
STRATEGY PHASE

One of my clients in the entertainment industry launched a new high-investment attraction at their venue every two to three years. Each time they made this huge investment, they observed a predictable lift in their revenue. Their business practically depended on capturing their target audience's attention every time they built a new feature in place.

However, throughout many years, the method they opted to use to release information to their audience was to keep everything under wraps until press day, which was when they released a fire hose of information all at once, without anyone expecting it, aside from a very few passionate members of their already-captive audience.

Right before one of those feature launches, they were ready to do what they had always done, and wait for their usual lift in seasonal ticket purchases a few months after, as their press day occurred while the attraction was still under construction.

As the client came with their plan, I had the opportunity to challenge them into a more strategic way of thinking. This was the big idea: What if instead of people learning about the attraction for the very first time on press day, we increased their expectation months in advance by strategically cranking the excitement up until they are left screaming and begging for the final reveal?

The client accepted the challenge of going about with the campaign differently, so we created and implemented a response-based strategy. With our help, they torturously teased their audience for five months. The result? The absolute best launch for a new attraction in company history, and the most pre-sale tickets ever sold after a launch campaign, which resulted in millions of dollars in sales in just a few weeks.

<u>This</u> is the power of strategy.

Strategy makes bland communication good, and it makes good communication amazing. It amplifies the value of your message until it is *irresistibly attractive.*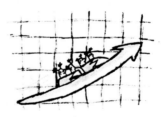

Knowledge of strategy also ensures that your message is received with the proper intention behind it, and that your audience responds as closely as possible to the way you desire.

There are countless ways to build a good strategy. Part of what clients seek from me is to do exactly this: Build bulletproof strategies that crank their revenue up to the limits. To set your expectations straight, I will not build a strategy *for you* in this chapter, but I *will* give you all the tools that I know and use to build extremely appealing, award-winning, and highly profitable strategies.

Think of it this way: If I were a famous chef, what would be more valuable to you? That I show you *a few techniques* that helped me cook one of *my* most popular dishes, or that I teach you my **most valuable techniques** so you can create *your* own great recipe?

In this chapter, I will teach you the components to build an outstanding digital strategy. I'll hold your hand at the beginning, just to link the previous chapter with this one; but then you'll have to pick up the kitchen tools and just begin cooking.

Let's begin; I'm getting hungry!

REHASH TEN BIG LESSONS

In the previous chapter, I asked you to write down the Ten Big Lessons you learned during the Discovery phase. Before building your outstanding strategy, let's take a look at these Ten Big Lessons once again.

Now, I'd like to ask you to write a response beside each of the Ten Big Lessons: What would be an action your brand could take to address that lesson?

These will just be very preliminary ideas, as at this point you haven't yet learned the strategic building blocks I reveal later in this chapter. I don't need your actions to be too strategic or tactical, just a loose idea on how your offer could address that particular issue you learned about your market.

For example, if one of your big lessons was that your customers are confused about a certain topic, one of your offer's action items could be to communicate and help clarify the topic for them. **Don't** focus on *how* the communication occurs at this stage. Let's focus only on possible actions from your offer towards your audience.

After you've performed this short exercise, you can download your Strategy Worksheet from here: www.cstps.co/StrategyWorksheet, before you move on to the next step.

OPTIMIZE YOUR OFFER

Another preliminary step we need to take is to once again clarify the terms of our offer. Hopefully, we've done most of this during the Discovery phase, but if we still have loose ends on our offer, this is the time to tighten everything.

After reading each question, fill in the corresponding checkbox in your Strategy Worksheet:

Do you have a clear description of your offer, placing a greater emphasis on what *your audience* is looking for, and not so much on what *you* would like to achieve?

Does your offer identify your target market with enough clarity?

Do you have a clear exchange of values for your offer? Is it for a price, another type of material exchange, or is it an intangible reward?

Do you have a method through which to deliver your offer?

Do you have average times in which the audience will receive what you are offering?

Do you have the rest of the terms that your audience needs to know before they take action on your offer?

Below the checkboxes, rewrite your revised

Product/Service Description, and right under that, the terms of your offer. Before the Strategy Phase kicks in fully, this is your last chance to decide to keep or modify anything in response to what came up during the Discovery phase.

It is extremely important to have absolute clarity on all aspects of our offer before building our strategy. Do not overlook this step, as nothing else in this chapter will make sense unless this is 100% squared away.

SELECTING A PRIMARY KPI

Part of what makes a strategy so powerful is that it gives us a roadmap towards a clear and objective goal or set of goals. We will refer to a sign that indicates whether we are moving forward or not as a Key Performance Indicator (KPI).

A KPI is essentially a metric that we will aim towards, and against which we will compare the actual results of our strategy in our last phase (Analysis).

Whether you define it or not, your efforts will have at least one KPI. I have seen huge budgets being completely splurged on campaigns where the only KPI was **to get it done**. Of course, we will aim towards a much higher standard than this, by ensuring that our KPI actively supports our offer.

Your strategy could very well aim towards more than one KPI. However, I would like to make two recommendations:

If one KPI correlates with another (i.e., if one KPI grows, the other KPI grows as well), consider placing those multiple KPIs in a nice hierarchy. This way, the goal of the strategy will have meeting the primary KPI as its main objective, with the understanding that the secondary KPIs will be met as a result as well.

If multiple KPIs do not correlate, and are rather independent from each other, consider building different strategies for each one. You don't want one KPI to suffer because of the strategy implemented to lift another KPI.

The five qualities that a good KPI should possess can be recalled by the acronym S-M-A-R-T:

Specific. The more well-defined a KPI is, the easier it will be to track progress and measure later on. Therefore, designing a strategy to meet it will also be a lot easier to do.

Measurable. It makes all the sense in the world to define a KPI in such a way that it can be measured later on. Numbers, percentages, and well-defined units are what we should strive for.

Achievable. Do not exaggerate the KPI. A goal that is grounded in reality and based on incremental levels of progress will be a much stronger foundation than one that is too aggressive or idealistic.

Result-Oriented. Make sure your KPI is a direct product of actions taken within the strategy. If the KPI you have in mind will be serendipitous, incidental, or completely out of your control, why even waste your time building a strategy to reach it?

Time-bound. Make sure you state time brackets for when you intend to reach the KPI, and when you will begin turning the gears to get there. A KPI without the goal to be met within a defined time period really tells us nothing.

KPI EXAMPLES

In the digital world, there are many different metrics that can be assigned as a KPI. I will explain a few of the most popular ones, along with a few rough ideas on tactics that you may use to meet or increase them. I explain tactics a bit further in this chapter, so don't worry too much if you don't understand each one fully yet. As you read them, consider which one you will assign as a primary target for your digital strategy.

Sales per Period. This is probably the first KPI most business owners think to measure, as it influences the bottom line somewhat directly. This is, quite simply, the number of sales that are closed in a determined period of time. *Tactics to increase:* Any of the tactics under "Sales."

Revenue per Period. Similar to the previous metric, but translated into actual gross currency amounts. *Tactics to increase:* Any of the tactics under "Sales."

Profit per Period. Similar to the previous metric, but after subtracting all costs. *Tactics to increase:* Any of the tactics under "Sales," as well as any effort to optimize all production costs.

Average Customer Value. As the name indicates, this one seeks to determine what the value of each individual customer is, on average. If your service is wildly variant on price points for different products, beware of this metric! You may need to break this down into types of customer for each product line. *Tactics to increase:* Upselling, funnel optimization, bundling, and others.

Visitors per Period. This is the measure of how many visitors land on a certain digital property during a specific timeframe. In objectives such as those found in an awareness campaign, this could be constituted as the final goal. However, if this metric is a precursor to others, such as sales per period, consider placing Visitors per Period as a secondary KPI. *Tactics to increase:* Any of the Audience-building tactics, as well as the Engagement tactics.

Average Subscriber Duration. If your business is based on a subscription model, this would be the average time during which your subscribers remain actively engaged as customers, that is, paying a periodic fee. *Tactics to increase:* Any of the tactics under "Engagement."

Customer Retention Rate. The percentage of customers who stay on board with your offer during a determined period of time. The formula to calculate this is: The total number of customers at the end of any period (CE), minus the number of new customers acquired during that period (NC).Take that amount and divide it by the number of customers at the beginning of the period (CB), and multiply the result by 100.

$$((CE-NC/CB)*100)$$

Tactics to increase: Engagement or Loyalty tactics.

ROI on Marketing. What was the exact return on all of your digital marketing costs? Calculate this easily by taking your total revenue minus total marketing costs, divided by the same total marketing costs. Remember to state your chosen time period. *Tactics to increase*: This one is tricky, but in very simple terms, the more a) costs can decrease, at the same time that b) sales/gross revenue can increase, the ROI will in turn increase.

Refund/Return Rates. The percentage of customers who ask for a refund or return, relative to the total number of customers. In general, decreasing this KPI should be a healthy goal to reach. *Tactics to decrease:* Aside from quality-control issues, which are worth mentioning yet not really the focus of this book, Engagement and Loyalty tactics may assist with this metric.

Shopping Cart Abandonment Rate. The percentage of customers who place items in their shopping cart but never continue on with the sale, relative to the total number of customers who place items in their shopping cart. *Tactics to decrease:* Funnel optimization, and other tactics under Sales.

Average Duration Until Purchase. The amount of time it takes for each customer to make a purchase, since their very first engagement with our offer. *Tactics to decrease:* Funnel optimization, as well as Awareness and Engagement tactics.

Value of subscriber. If your business has a free subscriber base for newsletters or other types of notification, this would measure the lifetime value in sum of all paying customers among the subscriber base, divided by the total number of subscribers. *Tactics to increase:* Any tactic that increases the number of customers among subscribers, or increases the average customer value, will positively influence this metric.

Earnings Per Visit. The average gross revenue per each visitor. In more clear terms, it's the gross revenue in a specific period, divided by the total number of visitors in the same period.

These are just a few of the KPIs that can be set as a goal to increase or decrease. Countless other granular metrics exist, which depending on your case might be good to keep an eye on as well.

Let's be clear at this point: We need to eliminate the idea that your strategy will have a nebulous goal of "a successful online presence." That may certainly be, in the end, a quality that our effective strategy produces. However, **always, without exception, our strategy will seek to influence <u>a specific</u> KPI.** *Do not* proceed to the next section without defining your primary KPI! The rest of this book may be informative, but will never actually *work* in a practical sense if this step is overlooked.

Now that we've looked at different types of KPIs, choose one of these to set your sight on as your primary KPI, and write it in your worksheet. This will become the main target for our strategy.

THE ANATOMY OF AN IRRESISTIBLY ATTRACTIVE STRATEGY

Too many online marketers jumble up every number of disjointed tactics and make the mistake of calling this a strategy. Some copy what others have done, and just shoehorn it into their particular scenario.

If you're following the methodology in this book, you won't make any of these mistakes, because you're taking a proven approach towards composing an irresistibly attractive strategy. You've also selected your primary KPI, and maybe a few secondary ones, so now you're able to determine which efforts will help move you towards meeting your goal.

Before we break down the elements we can incorporate into our Strategy, I want to take a moment to view in the big-picture what a strong Strategy looks like.

In the Digital BACON description of an irresistibly attractive Strategy:

Tactics: The specific actions that supports your strategy.

Strategic Scheme: The context in which your tactics take place.

Potential Competitive Exploits: The weak areas in which a competitor can be outshined or out-measured.

Our proposed anatomy, then, looks like this:

> An **Irresistibly Attractive Strategy** is **Based on Reality (Discovery phase),** with **Tactics** that exist within a **Strategic Scheme,** in order to conquer potential market share while considering **Potential Competitive Exploits.**

I see some of you with question marks in your eyes instead of pupils, but let's break each part down so it can be understood.

"An Irresistibly Attractive Strategy is Based on Reality (Discovery phase) ..." We already walked through the Discovery phase and filled in our Discovery Worksheet, which will be essential information for composing our Strategy.

"...with Tactics that exist within a Strategic Scheme ..." I explain this in depth in the sub-section about Strategic Schemes, further in this chapter. There's also another section where I give you an arsenal of Tactics. For now, you just need to know that tactics will vary slightly depending on the chosen Strategic Scheme.

"...in order to conquer potential market share..." Our ultimate goal is to take over as much of the market as possible.

"...while considering Potential Competitive Exploits..." Beginning with the sub-section following this one, we lay out six different weaknesses your competitor might have, which you can take advantage of in order to have an edge in your market.

What makes this particular combination irresistibly attractive?

☐ It is based on actual researched information versus flailing wildly to see what sticks.

☐ It's composed of carefully planned tactics within a scheme versus pecking away on random tactics without a contextual framework.

☐ It includes a concerted effort to exploit the competition versus running in circles and finding how much stronger the competition was *after* already being defeated.

A weak strategy usually overlooks one of these three characteristics. For the sake of everything you hold dear about your business, do **not** fool yourself into believing that you have a solid strategy until you can tick all three of these checkboxes.

POTENTIAL COMPETITIVE EXPLOITS

Pop quiz!

If you were the commander of a medium-sized army, and your task was to take over a city guarded by a much larger army than yours, which of these three would be the best strategy?

a) Take a few of your least-qualified soldiers, and ask them to enter the most heavily-guarded area of the city.

b) Take your whole army, and storm the city through an area which is guarded by a troop more or less the same size as yours, and hope for the best outcome.

c) Study the guarded city, find its weakest point, and exploit it with a small but highly-specialized group of soldiers.

Obviously, option a) will result in total annihilation and zero results. Yet this is similar to what happens when brands put forward a digital strategy almost exactly like their competitors, only much weaker — mediocre creativity, less compelling content, etc. They get annihilated because they are going against a much bigger competitor, using weapons that are way less powerful, so to speak.

Option b) *might* work, but it probably won't. Even on the small chance that it does work, it leaves your side weary and without much resistance against a counterattack. This is usually what we see occurring when the #2 brand in any industry tries to play the same game as the #1 brand. They use the same tactics, trying to win the battle by waving their features and benefits; but when the dust settles, they discover that they've spent themselves out in a short-term frenzy, yet have very little left to sustain an ongoing offensive effort.

It's clear, then, that option c) is the smartest. The good thing is that in the digital space, this might be easier to accomplish than in traditional offline marketing. Certainly easier than going to war.

You may very well be in an industry that has very low competition. If so, feel free to skip this sub-section, or you might want to use this knowledge to apply it to disrupt some closely-related industry categories through your brand efforts.

Below are seven possible weak points your competitor may be suffering from, which may be areas you can exploit — legally and ethically, I should clarify — to dominate your market. Also, you may find that the brands you're competing against are actually quite strong in one or more of these points, which will inform you on which are their "heavily guarded" areas, those through which you will choose not to send your soldiers. This will be very important information to keep in mind while selecting your Strategic Scheme as well as your Tactics. Both these sections appear later in this chapter.

Pull out your Competitive Analysis from our Discovery phase, and if you haven't analyzed each of these points, it might be a good idea to do so now.

Quality/Brand Strength. Some online efforts are simply mediocre in the way they present themselves to their audience, whether because of visual presence, or user experience as a whole. Stubborn business people get anxious about everything, except their identity.

How to find out: If you don't have the knowledge to judge a brand by its strength, or a Web presence by its quality, consult with a qualified professional in Web Design, Brand Development, Art Direction, or User Experience Design.

What to do about it: If your competition suffers from this common malady, your task will be to present your brand with a polished identity, as if *your brand were already #1*. Again, a qualified professional will be able to set concrete guidelines on how to outsmart the competition in this area.

Traffic Volume. A strong industry competitor doesn't necessarily mean they're receiving the most amount of traffic on their website. If you can capture more of the digital audience than they can, your brand could be on the right path towards dominating the market.

How to find out: There are several traffic-estimating tools out there. I sometimes use www.cstps.co/trafficestimate, and www.cstps.co/compete. On either of these, you can search your competitor's URL, and it will deliver a rough estimate of traffic received. It will also show you the main keywords your competitor ranks for. Compare the estimated traffic against the total volume of searches for those keywords. The wider the gap between those two numbers, the better the chances to exploit their shortcoming.

What to do about it: Any of the Audience-Building

tactics shown later on in this chapter will help you outdo your competition and conquer more traffic for your online presence.

Search Relevancy. Research suggests that the link in the first place of a search result receives 45-56% of the total traffic generated from that search result page, while the remaining 44-55% is sprinkled down among the other results starting with the second result.

If your competitor is not turning up in the first few places in the search result pages for your main keywords, there might be a chance for your presence to conquer this coveted spot. Even if they are dominating the main keywords, you might be able to find niche keywords related to your offer that they are not dominating.

How to find out: Simply search on Google or your favorite search engine for keywords of importance, and make note of which of them are dominated by your competition. Those that are not may be potential exploit opportunities.

What to do about it. The Audience Building tactics listed later in this chapter may help you climb up the search result pages. Paid campaigns could be helpful in the short term to appear in the keyword searches and attract traffic while any SEO actions take effect.

Backlink Strength/Weakness. Backlinks are links on external pages that point towards a website. In very simple terms, the more quality backlinks a site possesses, the more "authority" and "credibility" is passed onto the site by the search engines. Although this may change in the future, Google recently stated that backlinks are not going away anytime soon as their way to measure a website's authority and relevancy.

If your competitor's site is weak on authoritative backlinks, this means that even if they turn up in the first places of main keywords, there is an opportunity to beat them by having more high-quality backlinks than they have.

How to find out. There are quite a few tools to check a website's backlinks. As of the date I'm writing this book, the "Big 3" are:

www.cstps.co/opensiteexplorer
www.cstps.co/ahrefs
www.cstps.co/majestic

These sites offer paid account options for deep results, but they also offer surface-level results for free.

What to do about it. With the number of backlinks your competition has as a benchmark, now you know what to beat if you decide to go that route. SEO actions (not the focus of this book) can help here, but don't neglect strategic content and outreaches.

Customer dissatisfaction. If your competitor's current customers are so unhappy they're talking about it online, your brand can be the knight in shining armor galloping in to save the day. What they do poorly, you can do better, and this way dislodge them from the top spot.

How to find out. While you may never legally find out the complaints your competitor receives through their customer service line, you can definitely monitor websites, forums, and open social media channels like Twitter, Google+, and Yelp (refer to our section on "Social Listening" in the previous chapter). Use these to find out if they're griping about your competition, and if so, which exact subjects they complain about.

What to do about it. Once you find out the main sources of complaints, improve your offer to outshine them in these categories, and then use Audience-Building, Sales, Awareness, and/or Engagement tactics to make sure your brand can tout the fact that your offer is simply better than theirs.

Audience Engagement. A competitor could be above you in sales, but could be ignoring their own audience completely. If your brand is able to present itself as more conversational and open than the alternative, you might stand a chance to offer a more receptive experience, thus attracting more of an audience towards you.

How to find out. On Twitter, how many of their tweets are talking and announcing vs. replies? Make sure the competitor doesn't have a separate account just to reply to customers. On their Facebook page, are they responding directly to their audience's questions? On their blog, are they addressing and responding to people's comments? Just looking at these three items may give you a quick snapshot into how well they're engaging with their audience. If you find they're leaving loads of customer questions unanswered, that might be a good sign of an opportunity to do better than they are.

What to do about it. Choose one or more of the Engagement tactics listed later in this chapter, and interact with your audience as well as they deserve.

Unexplored Audience. Your competitor may be overlooking an important audience segment, which you can then come in and attract towards your offer. This is also called a "niche audience." Focusing on a niche audience may require you to change some terms of your offer, but it may be a more realistic goal than going head-to-head against a competitor that is strong in the other seven characteristics.

How to find out. Some brands let you know very clearly the type of audience they're targeting based on where they spend their advertising resources. Where do you see your competitors ads (offline included)? This can give you very clear cues as to who they consider their primary audience.

Two tools I like to use are www.cstps.co/alexa and www.cstps.co/quantcast. You can run a search for your competitor's URL, and check out their demographic information there.

What to do about it. Deploy one of the Audience-Building strategies targeted towards this niche audience. You also may need to roll back to the Audience Profile portion of the Discovery phase to fully explore this audience segment. A deep knowledge of this specific audience segment will guide every bit of content you produce, so it is important that you inform yourself as much as possible.

These are only seven out of many other weak points you may be able to identify. If you do find any weaknesses not listed here, by all means take note of them, and as you read the tactics list, think about which of them may be the best fit with which to exploit them.

STRATEGIC SCHEMES

I have to confess: I'm a big fan of Bruce Lee. He was such a cool guy, the kind of guy you would want as your best friend in school. You'd not only look cooler by hanging out with him, but he could defend you from bullies, probably by just staring at them!

One of the most famous Bruce Lee quotes is, "Now you put water in a cup, it becomes the cup; You put water into a bottle it becomes the bottle; You put it in a teapot it becomes the teapot. Now water can flow or it can crash. Be water, my friend."

Later I learned that when he said this during his infamous TV interview, he was actually quoting a line he recited (and apparently wrote himself) for a role he played in the TV show *Longstreet.* However, the idea preexisted him for centuries in Tao and Zen Buddhism philosophy. As  Westerners, we didn't really care where it came from. For all we knew, it was something Bruce Lee made up on the spot!

While our strategies cannot be like water — as it would defeat the purpose of having a strategy to begin with — one notion from this saying applies: Our strategies will take "the shape" of the recipient we put it in.

We will call these recipients "strategic schemes"

from here on.

A strategic scheme will contain and shape our digital strategy efforts in a similar way that recipients shape water. Our tactics will always be affected by our chosen scheme. The same tactic can be manifested in many different ways, depending on the strategic scheme we choose, just like the same type of fluid will be shaped differently depending on which container it's in. Think of apple juice inside a pitcher or inside a teapot. Same fluid, different shape. If you think I've taken the analogy too far ... It's Bruce Lee's fault!

Now here's the true nugget of wisdom: *Very probably*, there are already signs pointing towards the correct strategic scheme in the 10 Big Lessons we worked on at the end of the last chapter. They won't be obvious, but they will be subtly implied. Don't think of these as huge signs on the highway; rather, consider these familiar landmarks that you'll use to move towards your destination.

Beginning on the next page, I list and describe a number of Strategic Schemes. Before you read on, take some time to reread your 10 Big Lessons from your Discovery Worksheet. As you read through the different schemes, it will be obvious which of them aligns with what we learned during the Discovery phase.

Original Content. This scheme places content generation at the center of all strategic efforts. Content can be defined as information or creative material delivered through a type of medium, which can be text, visual, auditory, or a number of other types and combinations. Within this scheme, it is generally assumed that the content will be of particular interest for audiences to consume, wherein lies its value to attract and engage.

User-generated Content. This is a similar scheme to the above, with the difference that the content will be produced by the audience members themselves. There are many ways in which this type of content could be valuable, such as: empowering users, audience-building tactics, brand loyalty, among many others.

Gamification. Within this scheme, users are granted an experience similar — or in some cases, exactly like — a game, with metrics of progress and goals clearly stated.

Remarketing. This scheme has tactics addressing contacts which have already had exposure and/or engagement with our brand.

Database. This scheme hinges on the goal of not marketing towards the general public, but instead to a predefined segment, such as a contact list.

Contests. With an incentive towards a prize or reward, and a clear method to earn it, this scheme could be ideal to stir audiences into action.

Affiliate. The general understanding for this scheme is that there is a) a Vendor, who offers the good or service, and b) a Publisher, who markets the offer in exchange for a commission upon each sale.

Scarcity. The idea of this scheme is that there are a limited amount of opportunities, which will be communicated to the audience to spur action.

Word of mouth. This scheme is put in place with the understanding that testimonials and referrals will have a primary impact on the success of the strategy.

Viral. Though often assumed as easily achievable, a viral scheme assumes that the strategy will see an impactful increase in visibility, as a result of uniquely manifesting a message that is perceived as outlandish, shocking, perverted, revolutionary, or any among many other emotional triggers.

PR. This scheme relies on Public Relations efforts to carve the way into visibility and distinction.

Email. In this scheme, email communication is the core means, not only to communicate information with the audience, but also to motivate it towards action.

Event. Whether virtual or in-person, this scheme hinges around a specific moment in which audience members congregate — whether virtually or in real-life — and are engaged in a particular manner.

Drip. A series of specifically-tailored messages are send to audience members in a periodic fashion, each communicating a different aspect of the offer, or appealing to a different emotion.

Coupons/Discount. Within this scheme, audience members are given the opportunity to take advantage of the offer at a lower price, or with a greater set of features/benefits, than is normally available.

Sampling. The audience is granted a sample of

the offer, with the intention of captivating them with its benefits and leading them towards a purchase. It is generally understood that only a portion of those receiving the sample end up buying.

Trials. Audience members are given the opportunity to take a "test drive" of the offer before they fully commit to purchasing. It is assumed that only a portion of those taking the trial will end up converting into customers.

Mobile. The understanding that the desired audience can be primarily reached and engaged through mobile-enabled devices is at the foundation of this scheme.

Sales Funnel. In marketing, the notion of a "funnel" is a structured process by which we move our potential customers from a passive or neutral state into a positive sales action. The analogy of a funnel comes into play because we understand that at each step, we're qualifying our prospects, which means that some of them will turn away. We will then end up with fewer prospects, but ones with more potential for purchase.

One example of a common sales funnel scheme is:

KNOW (Awareness)
LIKE (Interest)
TRUST (Engagement)
TRY (Assessment)
BUY (Purchase)

Now that you've identified the scheme that best fits your offer, we'll discuss tactics you may consider placing within your scheme to form your own complete strategy.

TACTICS

One of the most unfortunate confusions that exists among people working on an online presence is that which exists between "strategy" and "tactics." As you've been reading up to this point, I have not used these two terms interchangeably, neither have I applied both labels to the exact same thing.

Many people who claim to know about online marketing refer to strategies, when all they really mean is "tactics." Some of these people never even *talk* about a strategy. Their efforts are so short-sighted! They think that deploying a random number of tactics is going to somehow transform into a strategic blueprint.

On the other extreme, some poorly-informed marketers speak about strategy, yet they don't know where to begin selecting the tactics that will work towards the desired outcome. They really only refer to strategic schemes, which are essential for us to begin from, but by themselves are too vague for us to take any action on.

In reality, tactics are the very specific tools, actions, and methods you will use to reach your goal. The strategy is the overarching plan that ensures your goals are met.

Allow me to use an analogy.

Let's say my goal was to solve the problem of my grass being too long and messy.

My **strategy** could be to get the lawn cut.

My chosen **tactics** could be to use my lawnmower on Tuesday afternoon, and my edger on Thursday afternoon.

Both the strategy and the tactics express an action towards the same goal; yet the strategy does not — and should not — describe the specific actions towards reaching the goal, while the tactics do not express the broader result seeking to be achieved.

The following is a list of Tactics you might select from to compose your Strategy. I will describe each one to some detail, and add a link to additional articles as warranted.

SALES TACTICS

This list of tactics have one thing in common: They help close or amplify a sale. All of them are rooted in traditional retail tactics, yet current digital tools allow them to take place without much complication and sometimes in a much more natural way to the consumer.

These tactics influence our audience during the purchase process, when to some degree they're positive about wanting what you have to offer.

Direct. Where potential customers are presented with an opportunity to purchase without any intermediary tactics. This is also referred to as "cold selling." If the offer is highly compelling or popular, this may be enough; otherwise, in most normal cases, it's usually considered an absence of strategy.

Upsell. A customer is presented with an opportunity to "upgrade" their purchase to one with a greater set of features, usually at a higher price point.

The customer can be presented with the upsell option right when adding the offer to their shopping cart, or even right before checking out.

Downsell. Where a customer declines to move

forward with offer A, and is then presented with an offer to purchase offer B which has a lower price. This ensures the prospect is not entirely lost without first making a sale, even though for a lower price. However, offer B could very well have a higher margin than offer A.

In order for a downsell to be offered online, the user must be presented with a clear interaction event where they positively decline the purchase. Only then does the downsell offer make sense.

Cross-Sell. Where a customer about to purchase offer A is presented with an opportunity to also purchase another offer, B, for a lower price. This plays on the customer's relative comparison ability. At the moment they're already willing to spend a greater amount, the lesser amount seems like a small incremental investment to make.

> The Web checkout process for Domino's Pizza offers you a chance to add wings or breadsticks to your pizza offer. Amazon also does a wonderful job of cross-selling right from each product page, in its section labeled "What other items do customers buy after viewing this item?"

Bundling. Where a number of different offers are presented, with the ability to purchase all of them for one price. This may be perceived by the audience as advantageous for several reasons: More convenient, a lower price than buying each one separately, added value to a purchase, saving on shipping costs, or any others. From our end, it could be a natural transition into an upsell offer (mentioned above).

> Amazon has a section right under most of their products labeled "Frequently bought together," in which they bundle two or even three other items along with the item the user is currently looking at.

Coupons. One of the greatest purchase triggers is a deal on price, and coupons often do the trick better than anything else. In the brick-and-mortar world, coupons are scanned via barcode; in the digital world, you have codes that you input which immediately slash the stated price in the user's shopping cart. This code can be promoted through other sites, via private messaging, or even through physical means such as store displays or postcards.

Price Comparison. Customers love feeling that they're getting a great deal. A price comparison chart between your offer and other alternatives could be a great way to express that your offer is lower-priced, greater in value, or both.

Scarcity. When most customers feel like they are about to miss out on a great offer, they tend to suppress the thought of leaving it for later, and they pull the purchase trigger sooner. Your tactic can be expressing a scarcity of time (Ex: "Offer only available for 24 hours"), or scarcity of quantity (Ex: "Only 45 units left").

> Ebay does a great job at expressing both of these notions of scarcity; of time, in their normal auction listings, and of quantity, in their other type of

listing where you can buy a number of units, while it displays how many of them are remaining.

Free trial. As customers enjoy feeling like they're getting something for free, they also like to feel like they have nothing to lose. One of the best ways to help them let their guard down is to offer them a free trial on subscription-based services. The longer the trial period, the less they feel there is a risk of being disappointed.

AUDIENCE-BUILDING TACTICS

This set of tactics is effective to motivate traffic towards your targeted property on the web. When visitation is the spark that ignites your strategy, choose one of these methods to make it happen.

Pay-per-click (PPC). One of the most basic traffic-generation tactics on the web, PPC ads are flexible to deploy, as charges will only be made according to how many users click on the ad. In order to maximize the effectiveness of this tactic, the ad should be as clear as possible to avoid people clicking for a confused reason.

PPC ads offer metrics on how many clicks are performed, which is great information to refine our campaigns for maximum effectiveness. Some of the most popular PPC ad networks are Google AdWords, Facebook, and a few others.

CPM (Cost per 1,000 Impressions). The "M" stands for "Mille," the Latin word for one thousand. These are similar to PPC ads, but this type of advertising charges you a certain amount per one thousand impressions shown. Although these ads "compete" for visibility in many of the same networks as PPC ads, you may want to consider which is more valuable to you.

Display ads. These are visual ads presented in various spaces over the web, and are sometimes referred to as "banners." These need to be visually compelling and have a strong message in order to drive users to click on them.

Retargeting (aka. Remarketing). This is an ad tactic that captures a behavior that links an individual web user with a site visited, places a cookie on their browser, and this way presents an ad related to that behavior on other websites. Retargeting ads generally have higher click-through rates than normal Display ads, although the cookie expires after a certain amount of time has elapsed.

Sponsored content. Certain sites, such as Twitter, Tumblr, and Reddit, have tools available to highlight certain posts of commercial nature. Use these carefully, as they should ideally be used for organic "conversational" type ads, not necessarily for hard sells.

Mobile ads. Most ad networks have options to display ads only to users navigating through mobile browsers. This might be ideal for certain types of advertisement actions, especially those which prompt users to take action right when they're at a certain location.

In-App Ads. Many ad networks allow exposure within certain mobile applications, typically those that are free for the user to download. The ad network usually shares a portion of the ad cost with the app developer. Lately, more visual, interactive, and even video ads have started appearing in ads in this way.

YouTube Ads. With a great majority of video traffic to its credit, YouTube has really taken off as an advertising-driven network in the past few years. Ads can appear as featured videos, banners (often with video within), static banner ads upon the video,and in-stream video ads (often before a video begins playing, which at times allows the user to skip it).

Squeeze Page. In cases in which contact information (often just email addresses) are sought to be collected, a common tactic is to create a squeeze page, which is nothing more than a page that has only one intended action: To "bribe" a user to provide their contact information in exchange for a download or additional content. The more compelling the "front" of the squeeze page (where the contact form lies), the higher you can expect the conversion rate to be. This is why many squeeze pages now include a lively video on the front along with compelling copy.

Free Content. Free content or resources can be excellent to get users to take action or just engage with a brand. The most common use is to collect contact information (just as in the case of squeeze pages) in exchange for content of some kind, but this tactic can be used to prompt other actions as well.

For example, the very cool Pay With a Tweet (www.cstps.co/paywithtweet) allows site owners to require users to send a Twitter message in exchange for something, such as an eBook, audio download, or font. This opens the possibility of other users seeing those tweets and visiting their site.

SMS Campaigns. Free incentives also can be given out in exchange for contacts' phone number, through which SMS messages can be sent. Some of these SMS campaigns allow further interaction through SMS or other means, such as users clicking on links to browse through their smartphones.

Organic Traffic/Content Marketing. There is a whole lot that can be said on this subject. For now, we can define this tactic as creating content based around what our users might already be searching for online, with the intention of satisfying their search through our content. This requires prior research for what they are already looking for, or might be interested in. The content developed should contain the proper keywords in its title, and preferably in other select areas in the content, such as the first paragraph, image "alt" tags, etc.

One of my favorite variants of this tactic is creating content for "long-tail keywords," which are those which are *not* the top searched keywords, but rather related searches that don't have as much search volume. For this reason, there is typically less competition for them, and cumulatively, they add up to a good number of searches. In some cases, long-tail keyword search volume added up can be as much — or even greater than — the most searched keywords.

Affiliates. One of the ways to bring traffic to your presence is by utilizing the audiences that other brands have already gathered. Your affiliates would get a percentage or flat commission on each sale generated from an individual they send.

In the same manner, your brand can be a publisher for another brand's affiliate program, and you would get the commission on each sale completed by one of the contacts you send over.

Email Newsletters. Email is still one of the hottest communication channels around, and users will give you permission to send them emails as long as you offer to give them something valuable in exchange. This is a great way to ensure you have a captive audience, that is already interested in your subject. Once they give you their contact, you have permission to send them newsletters and informative content. Obviously, you want to make sure you never misuse their information nor send it to others.

AWARENESS TACTICS

The list below shows tactics that amplify and help communicate your brand or your message, without necessarily expecting a purchase action, at least not immediately. Most — if not all — of the Audience-Building tactics can certainly be used for this purpose; however, we'll focus on a few that are specifically intended to create awareness.

Hashtag Movements. They may have started strongly on Twitter, but now that they're also heavily used on Facebook, Google+, Instagram, Pinterest, Vine, and others. **#HashTagsAreHereToStay.** They're a great way to categorize and promote your campaign content, so that you and other users on those channels can quickly collect related information about your movement. A good idea is to search on sites like www.hashtags.org before deploying your campaign, just to make sure the tag hasn't been previously used.

> Wendy's deployed their hashtag #PretzelLoveSongs to promote the return of their pretzel bun burger. They asked their audience to tweet and post lyrics to a love song for the burger. After the hashtag gained traction, Wendy's surprised their fans by hiring Boyz II Men to sing a song based on the tweets and posts received. (You can listen to the song here: www.cstps.co/pretzelsong)

On-site Web Content. Many brands have had much success by giving users the ability to pull up additional content (sites, interactive content, video, etc.) on their smartphones while visiting a certain location. While QR codes have been burned out to death, they are still an option to get users quickly to a website; however, a shortened link (like those www.bit.ly.com generates) might be more compatible for the majority of users.

Blogger Outreach. If you can give bloggers a reason to pay attention to you, they will. Don't try to be manipulative, as this will have no effect, and it's just not nice either. Flatter them with personalized content, or give a few of them something exclusive (even a physical reward is OK at times!). If you do this well enough, they might decide you're so cool that they will amplify your message on their own sites.

Video Assets. Many channels that allow video sharing are ideal for when brands want to create mass awareness. YouTube is naturally the first one that comes to mind, but Vine and Instagram also allow videos, though of limited duration; however, these can be quickly consumed and shared. YouTube does allow some level of additional interactivity with its clickable captions, while all of these allow interaction through commenting.

Of course, video assets also can be shared directly on your website, whether embedded from one of the aforementioned services, or placed directly on your site.

Visual Assets. Under the static visuals category, there are still many types of content that drive visitation and interest. Galleries, graphs, and infographics are still very much searched for by interested users, and if they perceive value from it, they are likely to be shared along as well. For visual content to work at its maximum effectiveness, the content needs to be useful, interesting, or just plain hilarious... or better yet, all three!.

> **Note:** Current content delivery platforms have made producing readable content very easy, but not everyone is producing visual and interactive content. Out of those who *are* producing these types of content, only a select minority are producing it in a truly remarkable fashion. If you want to stand out, your content plan should dedicate great effort towards producing visual & interactive at the highest quality you can achieve.

Cost Per View (CPV) Ads. Although this tactic could also be placed alongside the others under the

Audience-building tactics, because of its nature I'll include it here. CPV ads appear on some websites and videos as interstitials or pop-ups. As the name indicates, they charge you each time a user decides to view it. Some channels charge you only after the user has spent a minimum number of time watching. Depending upon the nature of your message, you might find this type of ad to be a powerful tactic for your arsenal.

ENGAGEMENT TACTICS

There's a saying that goes, "better have them say anything about you, rather than not say anything at all." If your goal is to get the audience engaged with your brand, here are a few ways to do it.

Forums. Contrary to some people's opinion, forums are in no way a thing of the past, as those that are centered around very specific communities are still alive and well. Generally, a new user that signs up just to sell their goods is frowned upon. If you know of any communities that have something to do with your industry, it would be a good investment to participate in the conversations, but please — do it as a human being, NOT as a brand! Be ready to give massive amounts of value, and respond to their concerns and questions sincerely. Of course, passively identifying your connection with your brand through a signature and your profile is absolutely fine.

On the other hand, there's nothing that says you can't begin and administer a forum of your own. Building the community will probably be the hardest step, but once that's going and they see value in that space, it could be a wonderful way to keep your audience engaged. Keep in mind, people generally hate joining a forum if they sense it's nothing more than a ploy to sell products. You need to offer much more value, and less shoving ads on people's screens.

Forum-like tools. Many social networks have built tools for forum-type discussion. Both Facebook and LinkedIn offer their particular versions of Groups; on Google+ you have Communities, and so on. The same rules and ethics that apply to traditional forums also translate over into these. The only additional point to keep in mind is that users in those spaces usually prefer content that stays within that particular social network, rather than content that forces them to click out and leave for somewhere else.

Reddit. This one is a beast of its own. While in many ways it possesses all the features of a forum, its upvoting/downvoting feature and Gold awarding — which translates into instant approval/disapproval from other users — make the most popular content and comments float clearly above anything else. Blatant commercially-driven content almost never succeeds, and on the contrary, very nasty things could happen as a result. You *really* don't want to know. Let's just say, things escalate **really** quickly.. However, the AMA (Ask-Me-Anything) posts have really taken off, with celebrities and even presidents participating in lively discussions, and those usually have an ultimate goal to generate publicity, although dressed up as satisfying people's curiosity about a certain subject.

Helping people sincerely is generally very well received, so that should be your first priority. Yes, that community loves funny (to say the least) content, but helping others should be at the top of your list at all times. If you can find <u>very</u> organic ways in which your offer can solve very real problems, be extremely careful about not pushing, but by all means offer to help other users.

Blog commenting. It's a great idea to read and comment on blogs centered around the topic of your offer. You often get the chance to not only interact with influencers in those spaces, but can also exchange ideas with other like-minded people interested in those topics. Many blogs will allow you to add a signature and even a URL on the comment, which is great to help identify yourself. The URL also may serve as a backlink to your site, although whether this helps your SEO in a concrete way or not is still hotly debated; however, if your comments are valuable enough, there's a high chance you might get some clicks over to your site.

Personally, I prefer sharing a link to the blog post on my Google+ profile, and then mention the name of the blog owner or author, and there I add my comment. From my point of view, this is a super-powered way to comment: You're sharing / curating good content, you're exposing the author to others who have you in their your circles, and you're adding your thoughts to the conversation.

Facebook Pages. Brand Pages are still being used heavily, although Facebook's crush on organic reach in users' News feeds has made many brands question the value of putting a great amount of effort into getting users to Like their page. Still, many users flock to a Facebook page to offer their testimonials and even ask for customer service, and you should not overlook participating and answering on behalf of your brand.

Twitter. In the same way, many users on Twitter @ mention brands to let them and their followers know what they think about the brand, which makes it a great avenue for real human interaction about topics.

Similar to my tip under Reddit, if you can find ways to organically help users through your offer, you might find that it will be well-received. One of my favorite power tips is to search phrases that people who need my offer might say, and store them on Twitter as Saved Searches. Then I can review these every once in a while, and respond to those that I think might be a good fit. I prefer following this tactic through a personal profile, rather than a brand profile.

Another trick is to find people putting down your competitors, and engage them about their experience. **You don't** want to slam your competition with those people, but given that they're open to have a discussion about their pain points, use that as an opportunity to learn how your brand can do better. And once again, don't stop if there's a chance for you to help them out!

Google+. While the "Big G" also has brand Pages, I've found that much better interaction occurs on the personal profile level. That doesn't mean you should abandon one in favor of the other. Both can be powerful methods to engage with your audience.

Not to surprise anyone, but Google+ has an extremely robust search feature which allows you to dig up related content, hashtags, and key words, and add your voice to those conversations.

Games. One of the most powerful ways to engage users is to gamify their experience, whether it's through games built around your brand topic, or by adding game functionality to other website functions. These can be functions like points, progress bars, rewards, etc.

In order for games to be successful, users need to feel that the experience was built with their entertainment or delight in mind. Moving a flying corporate logo around with a joystick is stupid, but if you can manage to convey details about your brand through a creative game, you might be on your way towards a winning combination.

> For the pre-launch of Harry's Razors, the company decided to wrap a referral system within a game, where they made different prizes available depending on how many visitors each user referred to their pre-launch site. To do this, they supplied each registered user a unique link, which they could then pass around via social media.

Tools. Did I already mention people on the Web are open to being helped? Traffic flocks towards places where people feel like they can get a problem solved — however small it is. One way to do this is to offer valuable tools with which they can interact and get something of value. If the tool is unique and helpful enough, the engagement might even lead to shares and additional traffic. A few examples of tools are: calculators, checklists, personality tests, and in general, things that offer valuable information that users cannot easily figure out on their own, or that return an interesting/funny/unexpected result.

Live Video. By offering a free live video service, Google+ (through its Hangouts product) has disrupted the market previously conquered by webinar and video-conference services. These still offer many great tools that are more advanced in nature. Most of these services offer simultaneous chat capabilities, which offer further engagement opportunities.

Contests. One of the most effective ways to attract audiences to your brand is to offer an incentive in the form of a contest of some sort. The possibilities of terms and incentives are too numerous to list here. User-generated content has become a hot means to get an audience active around a brand subject. As there may be regulations on certain types of contests, a consultation with an attorney is always recommended.

LOYALTY TACTICS

The tactics in this list can be used to keep your customers loyal to your brand. You wouldn't normally use these at the beginning, when you're just launching your online presence, but that doesn't mean you need wait a very long time to introduce them either.

Rewards. Many e-commerce sites have begun implementing rewards systems, where points are accumulated for each purchase made, which can be exchanged for cash discounts or other perks.

Rakuten.com does a great job of visibly communicating how many "Rakuten Points" you've earned when you make each purchase. They even let you "pay with Rakuten Points" during the check-out process.

Other offers, where some level of repeated purchases is expected, take the "punch-card" approach, which gives customers a greatly-valued item for free, or for a huge discount, once the customer has made a number of purchases, or has taken a certain number of actions. In a way, this is the "free trial" approach flipped over its head. For example, instead of saying "First month free," it's rather "Pay for 11 months, get the 12th month free."

Subscription perks. A "VIP subscription" that grants some kind of convenience is a fantastic way to keep customers buying from you and not from your competitor. Given that they're already paying you to remain a subscriber, they tend to feel that if they were to buy from a competitor, they wouldn't be taking full advantage of the subscription they're already paying for.

Amazon Prime is a great example of this tactic. Customers who pay an annual fee for their Prime service get free 2-day shipping, streaming movies, and many other great perks. Participants in this program are less likely to buy the goods that Amazon offers from anyone else.

Tiered Offer System. If your offer is a subscription

or long-term engagement, you can consider a tiered-pricing category system. These tiers can be labeled, "Bronze, Silver, Gold," "User, Pro, Enterprise," "Basic, Plus, Executive," or any others.

Where's the loyalty tactic here? For customers subscribed for a good period of time, they can be bumped up a tier for a limited time, and this way get to experience the "Gold Member Experience." This not only opens the possibility of increasing revenue, but also of promoting a feeling of gratitude from them due to the unexpected perk.

MOBILE TACTICS

Check-In Incentives. Although the concept of a check-in is not as innovative as it used to be, social media channels like Facebook, Google+, and FourSquare — which at the time I'm writing, is migrating its check-in functionality to *Swarm* — have continued to use check-ins as a way to help users announce to their friends that they are visiting a certain business or venue, and present them with a coupon or other reward.

SMS. Although we mentioned this medium under our "Audience-Building" tactics, SMS, also known as a text message, is still one of the cornerstones of mobile usage. People can opt-in for targeted messages, such as promotions, coupons, and other content delivered via SMS. You can also use SMS to send a link to special content or interactions. All that's needed is a service that assigns you a special SMS number, and when users send a specific word to that number, it will auto-respond with a pre-set message, including the ability to send along a link.

Mobile applications. More and more brands are deploying their proprietary mobile applications, with a possible list of functions that is too extensive to list here. This allows users to access additional benefits and conveniences related to the brand, as well as receive targeted push notifications.

Some of the best mobile apps are those that tie a business function into the smartphone's function. For example, a branded app can use the GPS to show how far a business location is from the customer, or can offer to add events directly into the user's calendar, etc.

Geo-Fencing. This tactic allows brands to draw a virtual "fence" around a physical area in the real world, which when entered by users, triggers certain smartphone functions, such as push notification or SMS message. Some brands have begun using this tactic as a way to send relevant and timely pro-motional messages to their potential customers.

Mobile search advertising. Although we've mentioned search engine advertising (such as PPC and CPM) under our Audience-Building strategies, it's worth mentioning once again that these same ads can be targeted only to users searching through their mobile devices.

EXAMPLES OF TACTICS IN PLAY

Once you've looked over the massive list of tactics included here, you may be wondering: How do these all fit together? Below are two examples of how some of these tactics can be strung together into a full strategic plan. I call these "recipes," as they are pretty much a collection of ingredients (Tactics) that amount to a larger recipe (Strategy).

THE EMAIL NEWSLETTER STRATEGY

Strategic Scheme: Email

Goal: To collect email addresses

Primary KPI: Number of emails collected

As you can see in the chart above, this strategy begins with a PPC ad that drives traffic to a Video asset embedded on a squeeze page. Once visitors watch the video, they may opt to sign up for another

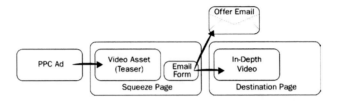

in-depth video with more content, by signing up to the newsletter via their email address.

This is a typical funnel strategy, as a portion of those who click on the ad will sign up for the newsletter, and a portion of those signed up will convert to an offer sent via email.

THE BIG AWARENESS STRATEGY
Strategic Scheme: Word of Mouth
Goal: To get people to sign up for a monthly donation, offered as two different tiers
Primary KPI: Number/amount of donations

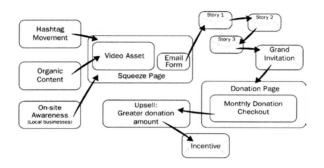

Here's an effective strategy that could be used by a non-profit or other type of organization looking to compel others towards action.

It begins with a few Awareness tactics, including a Hashtag Movement, Organic Content, and On-site awareness by a few local businesses. These all point towards a Squeeze Page with a Video Asset explaining the essence of the Non-Profit, and prompting users to sign up to a Newsletter via their email address.

A bit later, a series of stories are sent via email, ending up at a grand invitation to visit a special website where visitors are asked to donate a small amount via a monthly subscription. Once they donate, an Upsell to donate a greater amount is offered in exchange for an Incentive via email, thus converting a percentage of visitors to the higher-level donation tier.

THE MOM AND POP SHOP STRATEGY

Strategic Scheme: Mobile

Goal: To motivate people to come into the store when they're close by

Primary KPI: Sales (through trackable discount code)

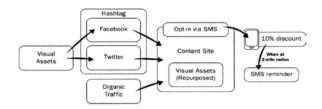

This strategy is a great one for local businesses. It ensures they are in the customer's mind, even when they're least thinking about them.

The business spreads Visual Assets via Engagement media, like Facebook and Twitter. The posts include a campaign Hashtag. It also includes a shortened, trackable URL to a content site, which is also pulling in visitors via Organic Traffic.

On the site, there's a highly-visible banner for customers to opt-in to messages via SMS for a 10% Coupon for their next visit. The opt-in not only incentivizes visitation, but also signs the user up for Geo-fencing. This way when they're at a 2-mile radius from the business, they get a text-message reminding them to stop by and take advantage of their discount code.

THE TICKLE-TEASE STRATEGY

Strategic Scheme: Event
Goal: To tease users before a big reveal
Primary KPI: Viewers for Live Video, plus social mentions of hashtags/keywords

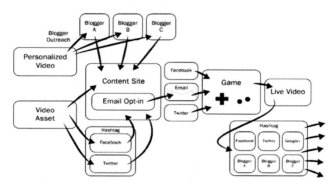

This is an advanced strategy that works great when businesses are planning a big reveal, but want to tease audience members beforehand.

First, Video Assets are published via a content site, as well as on several Engagement channels. Personalized Video Assets are shared with targeted bloggers to put a Blogger Outreach tactic in motion. The bloggers are asked to promote the content site, which also collects emails so that fans can be notified when further clues are ready.

Later, an Engagement tactic in the form of a Game is launched on the content site, which is promoted via Social Media and through Email Newsletters. The Game reveals teaser clues, and a date for a Live Video event.

On the day of the Live Video, the brand makes its big reveal, while they promote a Hashtag Movement to keep the buzz going well beyond that date. The bloggers who were engaged naturally report on the big reveal, and the buzz is amplified even further through their social and content channels.

ESSENTIAL COMPONENTS OF AN ATTRACTION STRATEGY

If your goal is to build an attraction strategy, it might help to take a look at three qualities that should be present in it: Your strategy needs to Reach, Pull, and Convert. As you design yours, make sure that you keep in mind a tactic (or a few!) that purposefully addresses each of these components.

Reach. No successful strategy can exist without reaching your potential audience where they're at. Even if they're already mingling on one of your existing spaces/channels, there needs to be one component that leads them into the entry point of the rest of the strategy.

The lower you set the barrier of entry, the more irresistibly attractive the reach portion of your strategy will be. For example, free content will always be more powerful than a purchase requirement; no sign-up will always cause a stronger reach than a sign-up requirement, and so on.

Pull. Once they've paid attention, you need to present something even more valuable, attractive, motivating, impressive, and/or memorable for them to engage further in your brand experience.

Convert. Unless your strategy is okay with passive awareness, you're usually looking for the audience to take some kind of action. Be explicit about what you want them to do, and put the tactics in place to cause them to step forward in your desired direction.

BUILD YOUR OWN STRATEGY

Hopefully, these examples have shown you creative ways to combine the schemes and tactics we just went over. In order to build your Strategy:

1. Review your 10 Big Lessons
2. Review your strategic goals.
3. Define your primary KPI.
4. Select a Strategic Scheme related to the primary KPI.
5. Define the Tactics to be used.
6. Combine the Tactics in a manner that affects the KPI in a direct manner (Strategic Blueprint section of your Strategy Worksheet).

Of course, even after the strategic flow is designed, there are many more details that must be defined. The two main ones — Production and Distribution — will be discussed in their own chapters further on.

So ... which one is the next step? In our next chapter, we will go over the *Production* phase, and examine what it typically takes to go from designing our Strategy to sending it out into the world to help us reach our business goals.

CHAPTER IV

Creatively Developed

PRODUCTION PHASE

Here's a little story: There was once a businessman who wanted to build a brand new store. He was passionate about his new store, so he decided that the following Monday he would do everything needed to make it happen.

When Monday came, he bought a random corner lot in town, and drove his truck full of bricks to the location. He hired the cheapest workers he could find, who began laying bricks without any sense of direction.

The businessman was excited. Even though the walls seemed like they were going to flop down at any moment as more and more bricks were laid, at least the walls were going up! When the final brick was laid, the businessman celebrated his achievement. Who cares about planning, research, strategy? Only construction was needed, and that's what he got.

His joy was suddenly cut off when he discovered the horror... There was no front door for customers to enter the building!

I know, this is just a silly story. Nobody would be so crazy to jump into a construction phase without

proper planning. Yet, quite strangely, this is what businesses do when they decide it's time to go online! No research. No planning. Just *production*.

If you haven't skipped anything and have been following along, this will not happen to you. You've already gone through an extensive Discovery phase, and have built out your selected Strategy. Now it's time to look at the third phase, Production.

As we defined at the beginning of the book, the Production phase develops the assets required to run our Strategy, in a creatively unique and technically accurate manner.

Because there are literally millions of strategies that can be built from the tactics and schemes we went over in the previous chapter, there is no way I can define a production process covering each and every combination. Therefore, this chapter will be a loose collection of articles about production from many different points of view. As you read, you should be able to determine which portions support your strategy, and use them as guidelines.

In this chapter, we'll cover the best timeline structure for a website, brainstorming methods, video production and post-production, among many other topics.

Ready to build? Let's go.

THE VALUE OF CREATIVE EXCELLENCE

Many companies producing Web assets feel like they can get by with poor creative output, which they feel drawn to because of lower monetary costs. Besides, quality doesn't really matter for sales... or so they think.

Centuries ago, in order for you to appreciate the creative genius of masters like Mozart or Rembrandt, you needed to a) belong to the highest levels of economic status, b) physically transport yourself towards a location where you were allowed to contemplate excellence, and c) arrive at the precise time and location when these pieces were being exhibited or performed.

Not anymore.

The Web is truly the great equalizer.

We live in a world where the most fascinating, outstanding, and admirable examples of creativity are at most people's reach, right from the palm of their hand, without requiring them to even step out of bed. Handheld, tablet and even wearable computers are becoming less expensive than ever before. Economic status is no longer a barrier, as anyone can go to a public library and access the internet for free, enter a museum on free days, connect at certain locations via free Wi-Fi access, etc.

It would be a violent crime against your brand to fool yourself into thinking that your audience can't distinguish between absolutely outstanding creativity and low-quality output. The apparent savings when ignoring this new standard results in a devaluation of your brand. Cheap is just too expensive.

Successful digital efforts incorporate an irresistibly attractive presentation quality. Your brand deserves nothing less.

CREATIVE KICKOFF

During the Strategy phase, we purposefully kept creative considerations out of the picture. Strategy and creativity are two essential components towards building an effective online presence; and when I mean *essential*, I really mean that one should not exist without the other.

(By the way, if you haven't read my short eBook "The Creative Strategy Manifesto," you can download it for free at http://CreativeStrategyTips.com. In that book, I explain very extensively why I believe businesses must communicate both creatively *and* strategically if they want to have any chance at succeeding.)

Many years ago, I read a very interesting study on how to memorize loads and loads of concepts. This was a summary of the technique: Start by taking two related concepts, and "gluing" them together in your thoughts. For example, if you were going to the store, and needed to remember to bring eggs and detergent, you would imagine those two items associated in some way.

The key to this memory trick, however, is the type of "glue" that stuck them together. The association between the two ideas needed to be as outrageous, hilarious, grandiose, exaggerated, morbid, scary, or violent as possible. Only these types of ideas stand out enough for our brains to elevate to a place where we can pay attention to it, above the boring information that surrounds us on a daily basis.

In our example, we would associate eggs with detergent by imagining an enormous egg the size of the Empire State Building, with hundreds of people scrubbing it down with lots of detergent to make it nice and shiny under the New York City sky. (Yeah... now try to forget *that!*)

The reason I bring this up in a chapter about creativity is that this "glue" is the criteria that produces memorable ideas that stand out, and for the exact same reasons. We pay attention to ideas that are different from what we're used to seeing every day, and those are the ideas we tend to memorize as well. Just look at the title of this book!

As we think about our concepts, we need to keep them in this direction. Our offer may not be fit for an idea like a giant shiny egg in New York City... but who knows? Maybe it will. "Boring" industries like car insurance were producing a ton of *blah* advertising, until GEICO came along and dared to make fun of itself a little bit, which has resulted in a ton of brand recognition and massive sales.

To be clear: I'm not telling you that you *must* go only in the comedic direction. All I'm saying is this: Dare to step out of the norm. One of the keys to separate yourself from the competition and create an *irresistibly attractive* presence will be to express how distinct *you* think you are. Can *you* become the BACON of your industry, or will you just be just another meat product at the grocery freezer?

MINDMAPPING/BULLETING

Now that we have our Strategy well laid out, let's once again go back to our Discovery phase findings, in particular, our 10 Big Lessons. What did we learn that can creatively inform our project?

Our goal here is to associate ideas and concepts to each of these 10 Big Lessons. Remember, we're not looking for strategies; those were already covered. We're looking for concepts that strengthen or enhance the bits of wisdom we found during our Discovery phase. What would be *attractive* to our target audience? What appeals to them right now?

One of my favorite activities to rock the creative juices is what people normally call "mindmapping." It's essentially a simple technique where words and concepts are laid out, and related concepts are linked to those freely. I find that it helps me associate many ideas to a root concept in a way that linear writing just doesn't manage to do (for me, at least).

I know many people prefer just writing lists and concepts in bullet points, which is perfectly fine as well. In my particular case, I feel like when I'm bulleting, my mind goes off in directions that really don't help my creative process. "Dangit, this list is getting long!" is probably what my mind screams most frequently.

However, when mindmapping, I get more and more excited as I fill the page with little bubbles. The key here is to associate freely, not to discriminate ideas quite yet. Later we'll have time to edit and discard, and quite frankly, most of what you put down will be pure silliness. Enjoy your silliness, take it in. Silly is the outer shell left behind when awesome is being born. *(I can't believe I just wrote that! Silly, right?)*

For mindmapping, you can use good ol' paper and pen, or you can use software like Freemind (www.cstps.co/freemind) and Xmind (www.cstps.co/xmind) , or one of the many available web-based versions like www.cstps.co/coggle. I enjoy drawing by hand in a notebook, and then I may redraw it in a software solution, editing and cleaning it up as I go along.

Here's how the mindmapping process might go:

In the center, draw an oval, and write a word or two that describes your offer. Then from that point, draw a line that connects to another oval. Within that new oval, write one of the 10 Big Lessons, in just 2-3 words if possible.

Then think of a few concepts related to that Big Lesson. If one of your Big Lessons is that your target audience is urban professional women, what are a few things associated with them, or that may appeal to them? Pop culture references, movie characters, jokes, related brands, all are accepted.

Afterwards, try and see if you can think of at least one concept — or better yet, more than one — to associate in the same manner from those new surrounding bubbles. At this point, you could be departing a bit too much from the central big lesson, but that's okay. Remember to go easy on yourself!

Anything good so far? Have you noticed any patterns, or any interesting associations? Now go on with the second Big Lesson, and repeat the same process all over again.

The main rule to remember in all of this is the following: **There are no rules.**

Once you've mapped out associations for all the Big Lessons, take a look at your mindmap. Aside from a sea of bubbles, what do you see? Any concepts surfacing that wouldn't have normally occurred to you?

Keep your mindmap handy, as you will refer to it later in this chapter.

OTHER CREATIVE PROCESSES

Just like the mindmap/bullet method, there are many other techniques that help bring out creative ideas. The most popular is probably the group brainstorming method. To apply it, you sit around with some of your peers, and blurt out ideas as they come to you, remembering not to critique nor filter them quite yet. Then, a facilitator or director writes them down, and at the end the best ideas are chosen outright, or modified in some way.

I actually hate group brainstorming, if I can be completely honest. I find that it's intimidating, and the process is biased towards those who have a natural knack for performing their ideas out loud better than others.

There's an alternative method that blends brainstorming and mindmapping. It consists of sitting around your peers — much like the brainstorming method — and handing out index cards to each person. Then, the facilitator reads a concept out loud, and each person writes the first idea that comes to mind upon hearing it.

After everyone finishes writing, each person passes

their index card to the right, receiving a new card from the person to the left. Then, each person reads what is written on their card, and writes a new associated idea below it.

The group then continues passing the cards along a few more times, until the index cards are completely filled. Then, each of the cards is read out loud. This produces ideas in pure "group-think," in a way that is simply not possible by one singular individual.

THREE MINDHACKS TO PRODUCE MORE CREATIVE IDEAS

I belong to the school of thought that affirms that each and every one of us has the ability to activate our creative mind. Nothing frustrates *me* more than a person who says they're a "frustrated creative." I feel like it's more likely that something — maybe even internally— have caused them to limit themselves, and not that they have some kind of genetic obstacle that blocks them from thinking creatively. As a matter of fact, I think most people disregard many small creative tasks they perform on a daily basis, including the way they move and express themselves.

My position is that by default, we're all born as creative beings. However, some of us need a bit more help to tap into our creative talent. Here are three techniques to jog your ability to think of fresh and new ideas.

1. Input stimulates output. When I was in advertising school and taking art classes, I reached a point where I felt a bit stumped in my ability to generate ideas. After taking a hard look at myself and my surroundings, I realized that I was making a critical mistake: I was discarding ideas too quickly, just because they didn't feel too familiar to me.

By "discarding," I mean that I spent absolutely no time considering whether there was any value in them. It happened to me with certain forms of art and music, with some dance styles (as an audience member — I'm a terrible dancer!), and others. If it was outside of my comfort zone, I showed no regard for it, even to the point of calling it "garbage!"

As soon as I realized my mistake, and corrected it by being more patient and consciously trying to find something good in *absolutely everything*, only then did my mind open up to new ways of thinking, and new perspectives.

This way, I infused my brain with fresh prime matter. In reality, that's all creativity is: a re-organization of previously perceived ideas. The more ideas I accepted into my mind, the more prime matter I had available to work with.

> **Mindhack #1:** Learn to observe the world around you without being critical, but rather identifying the positive aspects of everything.

2- Going for the unpredictable. Next time you're looking to create something, take the first idea that comes to mind, and put it on ice for a bit. Why? Because that first idea is probably what is most comfortable for you, and comfort usually signals that it's pretty normal to you already. Therefore, it has nothing to do with the new and fresh. No need to discard it completely, but just set it aside for a bit.

Now step out into the area you're *not* comfortable with. Even try to go in the complete opposite direction of the very first idea that came to mind. For just a bit, don't worry if the idea travels too far from your subject matter. Stretch yourself first, then whittle away until you land closer to the main subject, but from an unexpected point of view.

This exercise will help you break from your routine patterns of thought, and reorganize your thoughts in more ways than those your mind normally produces.

> **Mindhack #2:** Lay aside the first idea that comes to mind, and challenge yourself to see the task from a different perspective.

3- The Cross-Media Imitation Technique. As a creative purist, I hate plagiarism. Not so much because it's offensive to others — even though it is — but because it's offensive against one's own creative abilities. Why copy other people's work when you're able to produce amazing ideas?

However, I also have to recognize that nothing we create is *truly* original. We are constantly pulling from other sources, whether consciously or not (see Mindhack #1). Because of this fact, there is actually a technique to copy other people's work, while at the same time being 100% creative and original. It sounds contradictory, but hang with me here.

If I wanted to design a website, and took another website and copied it tit-for-tat, that would absolutely be plagiarism. However, if I found a source from another medium — let's say from music, literature, or even culinary art — I could extract the aesthetic qualities from that source and reinterpret them as visual cues for my website.

Remember, we're *not* going visual-to-visual. This is the whole point. We're looking to reinterpret one type of sensory input to a different type of sensory output. The idea here is to go audio-to-visual, taste-to-visual, etc.

For example:

- String quartet No 1 in D Major by Sergei Rachmaninoff: Sharp uplifting tones, small areas of color surrounded by empty spaces.
- *For Whom the Bells Tolls*, Ernest Hemingway: Direct images, down to earth and uncomplicated with emotional tones.
- Apple pie: Pleasant and sweet. Tactile, earthy, and familiar.

These are just a few qualities that occur to me with those sources, which definitely provide me with fantastic queues to follow with visual and even interactive ideas. Yours might be completely different, **which is the whole point!** By tapping into the unique way we each respond to a source, we're effectively creating something original from someone else's work... Copying *while* being original at the same time.

> **Mindhack #3:** Choose a piece from a different medium than what you're trying to produce, extract the aesthetic qualities your mind perceives from it, and apply them to your new piece.

Whichever Mindhack you decide to use, just make sure that you've looked at the problem or situation with fresh eyes and have generated enough ideas to pull from throughout this chapter.

TALLYING EXISTING RESOURCES

Before we take this great pool of ideas and turn it into something that can be seen, heard, and interacted with, we need to take a step back and take another look at our resources. This way, we'll be able to judge at what scale we can produce every element involved in our Strategy.

Notice that I wrote "at what scale," I'm not assuming you'll be forced to discard any element quite yet. If your Strategy calls for video, I wouldn't want you to freak out and throw away the possibility of producing some kind of video just because you're in a tight budget.

Obviously, you won't be able to produce a $15,000 video for $50. There are simply some sacrifices that need to be made. If $50 is all you have, you might need to settle with a nice-looking slideshow instead of a video.

The idea is: You can either scale your budget up, or scale your expectations down. If you try to do both — expectations up and budget down — you will either end up burning yourself or your brand out, or burning out other professionals. Don't be that guy!

Also, look at human resources, specifically from within your team. If you have any skills or talents within your team which you can use towards creative production, why not use them? For example, some of my clients have made the wise decision to have internal staff write copy and blog posts for them. As they probably know their company's culture better than anyone, this has worked out great for them.

Any skills you or your staff cannot help produce,

you may need to mark as something you'll need to hire a professional/contractor/agency for.

Before contacting a pro, make sure you can define the project as well as possible, and also make sure you have due dates clearly stated, plus an idea of your budget. The more informed they are, the more precise their proposal and project commitment can reasonably be.

If you have a dollar amount you simply can't exceed, my best advice is to communicate it to the professional. Many people avoid giving out their maximum budget allowance for fear that the professional might gouge them. Now, while I can't affirm that there are no people out to gouge you for your money, I can say that a professional you trust or has good references will more than likely act with integrity. It's in everyone's best interest to have open communication from the beginning.

If your budget idea is too low, the professional should be able to advise what you can get as an alternative for your amount. On the other hand, if your budget turns out to be too high, they should be honest enough to tell you what additional deliverables you can get for that amount, aside from what you primarily reached out to them for.

Let's talk a bit more about pre-production considerations, before we get into the actual production tasks.

PRE-PRODUCTION

"Ready, set ..." In a race, before the runners sprint off at maximum speed, there is always a lead-up. During this period, runners get into a flexed launch position to reduce the curve of acceleration as much as possible.

This is similar to what happens right before a Production phase. During our pre-production period, we seek to collect and organize everything needed so that our actual Production phase moves forward without bumps or delays.

Let's begin by discussing the main resource in Production: Time.

PRODUCTION TIMELINES

Time is the most important resource we have, and it's the most delicate one as well. Money lost can be regained; time lost, however, is irreparable. This is why it's so important to carefully plan our timeline.

First, we should take a look at our selected strategy, and write down a list of all the assets that need to be produced to launch it successfully. Beside each one, write down an average of days needed for each of these assets to be completed, from beginning to end. If you don't have a rough idea on how many days an asset takes to produce, consult an experienced professional.

From here, probably the best way to map out a timeline is to use "milestones." Looking at our calendar, we'll set our final milestone — representing when we absolutely must go live — at a specific date. From there, we need to map out secondary milestones for each of the other assets. Here, I'm assuming that the live date *is not* the same date of completion for the assets. You absolutely want to make sure there is at least a day or two in between asset completions and a critical milestone like a live date.

Be cognizant of assets that depend on one another. For example, a website may require photography and copywriting to be complete before other tasks can move forward. This should be taken into account when laying down our milestones.

Once we have our secondary milestones, take each one and count backwards the amount of days you set on your list. You may or may not count the weekends, depending on your resources and comfort level, more on that below.

If you've managed to count backwards for all of them, and you haven't gone further back than the present date, congratulations! You're pretty close to putting together a solid production timeline.

However, if you *do* go further back than the present date, you may need to consider a few options:

If you were trying to avoid working over the weekends, you may need to reconsider this. It's better to work over weekends than to pretend you'll have enough time, when your timeline is clearly screaming that you don't.

Are there any more resources — human, software, hardware, or services — you can add to accelerate some of the tasks? Be mindful of additional administration tasks when more people are added, and of course, additional costs.

You may need to simplify some of the tasks. For example, for an asset that takes five days to produce, how can it be simplified so that it only takes three days?

In the worst case, you may need to drop an asset from the strategy completely. If so, ask yourself which asset you can eliminate without creating a domino effect that makes the whole strategy come apart.

Also, remember to leave periods of time for approvals and revisions. Nothing in production is ever absolutely perfect the first time around. Allow for some time to make amends as necessary. If there will be a particular person or group in charge of final approvals, make sure that their cutoff dates for feedback are clearly communicated.

Once you've assigned milestones for each asset, and have drawn out the production timelines for each of these assets, as long as everything looks realistic, you're ready to continue on towards the actual production.

Pro Tip: Don't try to fool yourself! It's a mistake to begin a plan knowing that you won't make the cutoff points. The end result will be money and time wasted.

Just know that in more projects than not, many issues along the way will require going back to review and tweak the production timelines. This doesn't mean that building the timeline was a waste of time. Editing something that exists is better than winging it along the way with no plan.

This has been a very quick overview of how to put together a production timeline, but the topic of production timelines doesn't end here. I've written an article with the typical stages of production for many different types of assets. Check it out here: www.cstps.co/howtoproduceassets

DRAFT PRE-PRODUCTION FORMATS

One of the best practices before any actual production is performed is to build mockups and draft versions of what will be the final items to be distributed and published. This allows you and your team to observe the creative output at an intermediary stage in between the raw idea and the final product.

There are many different types of pre-production formats, depending on the asset to be produced. Below I'll list the different final outputs, their corresponding draft formats, and how each one helps.

FOR COMMON WEBSITES

Sitemap. In order to understand the breadth of the site, and how the elements are connected to each other, a visual sitemap really comes in handy. This chart will mainly consist of nodes describing each of the user's landing points on the site, and optionally the assets included in each of these points. Then, lines and arrows will be drawn to describe how each landing point is connected.

A sitemap not only helps to understand the big picture of a site, but also helps to avoid forgetting important content at the last minute, failing to link certain elements, or helping to consider consolidating some of the content areas.

Content outline. A compilation of all the text content appearing on the web is a helpful measure to take, rather than writing all the content directly in the code or even our content management system. This does not need to be fancy in any way; in fact, the more detached from style elements the better, as it will help you and your team keep focus on the content quality by its own merits.

With shared text processors, such as Google Drive and others, you and your team/clients can have access to the same content repository in real time as you work along to collect and create content.

Moodboards. In order to express a desired "look & feel" for a brand, a collection of images swiped from other people's work can be put together on one board, which is usually called a "moodboard." These can either be swipes of the same media we are working on, in this case, interactive examples, but also can be samples of other media that provide inspiration, including fashion, architecture, photography, illustration, and others (somewhat like we previously indicated in our Mindhack #3).

FOR APPLICATIONS (AND MORE COMPLEX WEBSITES)

Flow diagram. The goal with this is to describe how your users "flow" from one space to another; be it a page, a dialog screen, action item, etc. Similar to the sitemap, this will consist of nodes and arrows. The difference, however, is that here we are not simply connecting items, but rather describing the different paths a user can take when cruising through your app or site. For example, if the user encounters a "yes" or "no" decision, we need to describe what they are presented with after each of those.

If there will be an administrative component of

the application, a separate flow diagram should be built to describe this experience as well; an administration panel requires as much of a user experience exploration as anything else.

FOR COPY

Drafts. Copy may go through several revision stages, depending on volume and approval processes. For web copy, usually the best practice is to begin a working document with all important keywords at the top, and a draft iteration of the copy right below it. This way, if other parties are to review it, they are immediately aware of any target keywords that are purposefully being included, and can make any revisions around them.

FOR AUDIO NARRATION

Scratch track. Before recording in a studio with a professional talent, the producer may opt to record a scratch track, which is nothing else than a vocal recording by someone other than the final talent. Scratch tracks serve a few purposes, but the main two are: 1) to measure the required duration to read the current copy, and if necessary, make any revisions to copy before recording, and 2) to allow any other production members that need to sync to audio to begin their work, way before an audio recording date.

For this reason, the scratch track needs to be as precisely timed and with the closest intonation as the final talent will be directed to perform. Even if it's not exact in timing, as long as it's close enough, the scratch track will serve its purpose.

FOR VISUAL BRANDING ELEMENTS

Sketches/draft iterations. Sketching out a logo or other branding element with pencil and paper allows artists to think very quickly about different directions in which to take the concept. This also allows all the deciding parties to be comfortable with the concepts, without investing too much time at the front of the process. Once a direction is identified as the right one, a refinement phase may begin.

Sketches may or may not include color. My recommendation would be to include color only if absolutely necessary for the particular goal being pursued; otherwise, gray pencil sketches are good enough to visualize the concept at this stage.

Color palette. A guide on which colors will be used throughout the project — whether for logos, interface elements, or any other elements — is one of the backbones of a consistent visual treatment. A color palette is not just a selection of colors, but *a system*. Each color must make sense on its own for a particular use, but must also work alongside the others.

A basic palette typically doesn't involve more than 5-6 colors. Obviously, more colors than this are acceptable in some instances, but any additional colors will typically be variations on the foundational 5-6 colors in our palette.

My favorite color palettes will be presented in some kind of layout indicating the proper *proportions* for each color. You will find that the same color palette can look very different when one color has been assigned a larger spatial proportion than another. For example, a color palette involving yellow, black, and orange will look much different if the larger fields are black with yellow and orange as secondary elements than if the larger fields are yellow with black and orange details.

Typography. A good style direction also will include some kind of guideline in regards to the fonts to be used. There can be many different approaches, but in general terms, a specific font is chosen for large headlines, a different one for titles, and another one for large bodies of copy. Another approach is that instead of choosing different fonts, different weights and sizes of the same font can be assigned to each function.

As in the discussion on color palettes, these font selections will be systematic. Each font must be in complete harmony with the others, and of course, must also reflect the brand personality. This is why I recommend thinking about typographic systems during the pre-production phase. It's helpful to just lay out the font directions on a page/screen, and judge whether they visually play well with each other.

If the web assets will have the ability to pull from an online repository — such as Google Fonts or Adobe Typekit — it's important to find this out before selecting fonts. This way, the font selection doesn't have to be more limited than it needs to be.

FOR VIDEO

Scripts. Video production scripts usually display two columns: one for audio, sound effects, and narration; and the other for descriptions of visuals. A third column may be present as well, with special production notes that won't necessarily be featured audibly nor visually.

Style frames. Usually in tandem with the storyboards, one or more finished frames may be built, which give an example of what the final production design will look like. These will typically have most of the key elements included, such as typography, color palettes, lighting, character elements, etc.

If the production will include live action, these may be painted, and is often called "production design."

Storyboards. Most people are familiar with storyboards: Rough drawings of key frames and elements in the video. The goal with these is to plan the different camera angles involved, in sequence. If the camera will be moved somehow, the best storyboards will add arrows to reflect this movement.

Storyboards for animated movies might be a bit more defined and with color, representing more frames throughout.

COLLECTING ASSETS

Before heading into each phase of Production, you will need to make sure that the prerequisites to develop each element are met on time, and that their quality and adherence to the original creative goals and brand guidelines are met.

For example, before going too far into the web design phase, are the sitemap and content outline completed and approved? Before developing the video assets, is the script finalized, and if a scratch track is required, has it been recorded? Before going in to code an application, is the flow diagram completed, and does it make sense with respect to the functional goals that were originally set?

This level of coordination will be crucial in order to guarantee that each individual production kickoff is launched correctly.

HOW TO PRODUCE YOUR ASSETS

I've written an extensive article describing the production process for most of the assets that will be used in your digital strategy. I've also added some of my best creative tips to develop each medium at the highest level.

Even if you're planning on hiring a professional to produce these for you, it would be in your best interest to be familiar with the typical production processes. This way, you'll be familiar enough to communicate with them in a knowledgeable manner. Check out the article here:

www.cstps.co/howtoproduceassets

HOW TO GET VISITORS TO DO
WHAT YOU WANT THEM TO

Many businesses have problems obtaining a good conversion on their digital campaigns. They feel like their offer is not compelling, or that their visual presentation may be off in some way. Quite often, however, it has nothing to do with any of these, but rather the absence of a powerful trick to make users take action in the way the businesses desire.

This trick is so deceivingly simple, that I'm bound to disappoint you when I reveal it below. You will think it's the most obvious thing in the world, yet 9 out of every 10 websites I visit still fail to implement this trick.

So what is this secret trick? Simple:

Tell them what to do.

Please don't underestimate the power of this trick — which is more than just a trick. In fact, it should be a guideline for *anything* you do with regards to presenting your offer in the digital space. I know it sounds like the most obvious thing to do, yet I will assure you that if you do not take it seriously, you are bound to get busy and *will* forget to apply it.

Let me explain: There are four major ways to present what is commonly known as your "Call To Action" (CTA) prompt:

Weak (the way 9 out of every 10 sites do it): Offers no compelling reason for users to take action.

Strong: Is phrased in an imperative tone, almost scolding the user for considering not taking action.

Organic: Is expressed in a natural and conversational manner, fully integrated into the tone of the rest of the content, yet highlighted from it.

Irresistibly Attractive: Gives one or more compelling reasons to take action, and lets the user feel they have nothing to lose, and much to gain by doing so.

Let's say, for example, your CTA tells users to sign up for a webinar, and you're placing this copy on the "registration" button. Here are the four ways you can phrase the CTA:

Weak: *"Sign Up ..."* Booooring! Everyone uses those words.

Strong: *"Click Here Now ..."* Effective, but a bit too demanding. Nobody wants to feel like they're back in elementary school. Besides, it sounds like Captain Caveman.

Organic: *"Reserve Your Spot ..."* Works great, as it tells the user what they are doing by clicking on the button.

Irresistibly Attractive: *"15-Second Sign-Up ..."* Then in smaller font: "Limited spots available".

I'm sure you're wondering: Why do I say that the last one is irresistibly attractive? There are two reasons.

First, which of us can't spare 15 seconds to sign up for useful content? It makes you feel ridiculous to turn down such a low barrier towards entry. Second, because the item in smaller font taps into our fear of missing out, also known as the *scarcity mindset*. So by phrasing it this way, we are not only letting them know that it would be absolutely ridiculous to leave this very small task for another time, but also informing that *there may not even be* another time.

Out of the four CTA styles, I suggest you compose yours as close to #4 on the list. In other words, a Strong CTA is preferable than a Weak one, an Organic CTA is better than a Strong one, and an Irresistibly Attractive one is more effective than any of the other three.

In the end, however, the absolute best CTA is — no

surprise — the one that works the best! In our chapter on *Analysis* I tell you a few ways to determine this.

HOW TO WRITE HEADLINES THAT HOOK

One of the most important elements when writing copy is the headline. It is said that 80% of users read an article headline, but only 20% read beyond that. Although they've been used since the beginning of the newspaper era they remain a very essential component to digital content today. Headlines are still fundamental, and they're still very functional.

Although there are many uses for a headline, the two most widespread are in articles/blog posts and in emails. The goals for each of these is very specific, so let's deal with them separately.

HEADLINES FOR ARTICLES/BLOG POSTS

When publishing an article or blog post on the web, the three goals of a headline are:

1. To give readers a very quick and summarized idea of what the article is about.
2. To capture people's attention, enough that they are compelled to take action and read.
3. To help search engines index the article under relevant search terms.

If you take a close look, Goal #1 is only dependent upon you as the editor/publisher. It is your responsibility to express the idea of the article in the least number of words as possible (55 characters is the ideal article headline length).

On the other hand, Goal #2 is only partly dependent on you. The part you can't control is what motivates your audience. You already have enough insight from your Discovery phase about what compels your audience to take action. The part you *can* control is the level to which you adapt your message precisely to what moves your audience.

Finally, Goal #3 is the one that is the least under your control. The search volume for certain terms is what it is. From the Keyword Research portion of our Discovery phase, you should have enough data about what words people are using when searching for your subject matter. Therefore, you can use these search terms in your headline to make it relevant to them.

There are many tips and tricks to writing a compelling headline, but beyond anything, your headline needs to accomplish the three goals above. Failure to meet these will result in readers not clicking through to read your article, people clicking but never reading the article, or articles that are never indexed by search engines under relevant search terms that have a significant search volume.

Here are a few headline styles that attract audiences irresistibly ... like BACON:

IMPLYING SOME HIDDEN, RARE KNOWLEDGE Nobody likes to feel like they're ignorant, so these headline styles make users feel like they have an itch that only your content can scratch. Some examples are:

A big secret about _____ nobody wants you to know

One thing very few people know about _____

The truth about _____ that nobody is talking about

The top lies people have told you about _____

HELPFUL OFFER People on the Web are drawn towards

resources that can assist them in some way, and even more so if the help is in the form of free content. The more confident the offer for help sounds, the more effective it will be. Some examples are:

The sure-fire way to get done with _____
Want to get rid of _____? Use this method
Try this and you'll be able to _____ today
How _____ made me a better person

CONVENIENCE Similar to the previous tip, this one also offers help, but makes it very clear that the solution will be easy, quick, and/or inexpensive to implement. Stating that it doesn't require a large investment nor risk helps overcome people's laziness — or skepticism that it might work for them. Examples include:

Apply this quick tip and get _____ done today
An amazing trick to overcome _____ in 30 minutes or less
The easiest way _____ can help make you a better person

NUMBERED LISTS People love to get a sense of the density of content they're about to open, before they actually open it. One way to ease their sense of uncertainty is to give them a number. This appeals to people's logical thinking, and makes them more likely to read on. Examples:

10 amazing places to _____ you just can't miss
The top 8 things to do after _____
The 15 best _____ in the world

Pro Tip: This one annoys many people, but it works beautifully. Do you want to superpower your Numbered headline? Make a reference to one of the

items on the list as a teaser. Examples:
10 amazing sites in _____ you can't miss. Number 7 is unbelievable!
The top 8 things to do after _____. I do #5 all the time.
The 15 best _____ in the world. Number 11 is just crazy.

WARNING People are attracted to information that can prevent them from making a huge mistake. Some examples:
The top mistakes people make when _____
This sneaky issue with _____ is costing you money
How _____ could get you in big trouble
Why you need to do something about ____ before it kills you

APPEAL TO CURIOSITY If you dangle the carrot, they'll run to you. One of the strongest carrots for readers is a headline that appeals to people's natural tendency towards being curious. In this style, you don't even need to be super-specific; being a bit vague is part of what makes people think, "What? I just need to know!" A few examples:
You won't believe what happened to this man when _____
You probably never knew _____ was a problem, until now
What _____ really means
If you read only one article about _____, make it this one

CELEBRITY COMPARISONS This uses a known personality to draw in people's attention about something else entirely. Be careful with this one, as making the connection too contrived could backfire. For example:

One thing about _____ that is more shocking than a <u>_Celebrity_</u> concert

A tip that will make your _____ look cooler than <u>Celebrity_</u>.

One thing about ____ that is scarier than dating <u>Celebrity__</u>.

Why <u>_Celebrity__</u> will never be good at _____

APPEAL TO THE DARK SIDE Yes, that was a Star Wars reference, and I'm a geek. But let's admit it: We all have a dark place within ourselves. These headlines appeal to that naughty child we're too ashamed to admit we wish we were, if only nobody were looking at us. Examples:

A few _____ you can totally steal today

How to cheat your way into _____ and still feel good about it

How to take revenge against people who _____

EXPERTISE Even if you're not an authority, as long as you imply that you're amplifying the opinion of experts, your headline will attract people's attention. Make sure your content can substantiate the claim! For example:

One thing most doctors agree about _____

Why _____ is making most experts very concerned

Researchers have agreed on _____ and it's not what you would think

OPEN-ENDED QUESTIONS This one has been used a lot by traditional media, but it seems to have carried over in digital media. It's similar to the appeal to curiosity, but these ones do it in a way that promises an answer

if we read on. Examples:
Is the end of _____ about to hit us?
Should you wear _____ to school?
Do you really need to _____ every day?

MEDIA CONTENT If your article contains media of some sort, it should be distinguished from any regular old blog post, as this normally gives the content a greater level of value. This should ideally be stated in the headline in some way, and special characters around it are normally acceptable. For example:
[VIDEO] Headline goes here ...
Audio Interview Tips to better ...
|| Infographic || The state of our nation ...

As you may notice from the format of my examples, I do recommend normal sentence-case for headlines Rather Than Typing Every Word In Upper-Case. Why? Because most people who share articles on social media are too lazy to change the headlines, and people tend to click on links that appear con-versational over those which seem like they're just promoting articles. Yes, this is a sneaky technique, I know. In the end, we *are* promoting articles, but we don't want this fact to stand in the way of people interested in our content.

HEADLINES FOR EMAILS

While the headlines for articles have their own goals, email headlines, or Subject lines, as they should be more correctly referred to, serve a completely different purpose: To cause the recipient to open the email.

And that's it.

If a recipient doesn't open the email ... the campaign is dead, at least for that person. You need to make sure that the subject compels them to open it right away, **never** to leave it to read later, something that will <u>never</u> happen. I have 29,260 unread emails in my inbox that prove this fact!

Below I've listed the top types of email subject lines that make people just *need* to open it. You might notice some overlap with the list above, but be assured, this is a completely different format. Here they are:

VAGUE DOPE As much as I hate this type of subject line, I end up always falling for it and open them. It's the kind of subject that sounds like the sender is a character in a bad reality TV show. It has its certain uses, but if you abuse it, you may get unsubscribed from pretty quickly. Examples:

Whoops, I goofed up ...

They told me not to ... I should've listened ...

This made me SO angry ...

Dude, I thought you were different ...

DIRECT SALE Almost the complete opposite from the previous type, this one wastes no time to let the recipient know what's up. The problem with this one is that a lot of companies opt to only use the direct line, so you run the risk of not differentiating enough from every other offer. However, if you know your audience is expecting something specific from you, there's no reason to beat around the bush. These examples will seem familiar to you:

Get 15% back when you spend $125 ...

The one sale you've waited for all year ...
Up to 70% off on _____ ...

SCARCITY People hate feeling like they've been left out. One of the ways to subtly imply that the bus is about to leave the station is via scarcity triggers such as:
Last 24 hours! Don't miss out ...
Two days left on our biggest buy-one, get-one free sale ...
Only 100 spots! Reserve yours now ...

SHOCK AND ROLL A sure-fire way to call people's attention is to give 'em a good old shock. They can't believe someone would dare to send them an email with those words, so they must open it to find out what could possibly motivate them to do such a thing. Even when you clarify what the subject is immediately after the email is opened, it still works. Examples:
Your neighbor is watching your wife: Today's Surveillance Culture
"I enjoy slapping women" - the psychology of a domestic abuse perpetrator
We tied our boss up with zip ties ... 50% off for everyone!
Disclaimer: I don't advocate peeping, domestic violence, nor tying bosses up in zip ties! Keep this one humorous or unexpected, and please don't abuse it (no pun intended).

APPEAL TO THE DARK SIDE Yep, this angle also works for email subject lines. Most people have a hidden Dennis the Menace complex that they give permission to come out and play when privately checking their email. Examples:

Steal my Special Report ... While I'm not looking!

How to hack your way in (not available to the public!)

A sneaky way to _____ (c'mon, nobody needs to know)

NUMBERED LISTS People like to check their email, but they hate the idea of wasting their time. If you state how many of something you're delivering, it's more likely that they'll check in to what you have to say. This usually works best when the number is stated as the first, second, or third word. Examples:

8 tips to get rid of that pesky moisture odor ...

6 foolproof tactics to grow a chia Mohawk this year...

The top 5 ways to breed Gremlins inexpensively ...

MEDIA CONTENT If your email includes a link to a specific type of media content, you will want to state this at the very beginning, as it separates your email from every other item in your audience's mailbox. Special characters might trigger spam filters, so I advise against using them in this instance. For example:

Video interview: Tips from a successful entrepreneur

Audio Podcast: M. Bison talks about being a top leader

Helpful Infographic about what works in astrological pottery

OPEN-ENDED QUESTIONS Cliffhangers just make people

itch for watching the next episode. Although the answer to most open-ended questions is usually just a plain "no," most readers can't resist to find out the reason why not. Examples:

Are squirrels about to cause the end of the world?

Does the recent news about cable companies mean we're all going to get sued?

Is A. Orange the new Messiah?

As in anything, it's never a bad idea to mix things up. In other words, never send just one type of email subject line. If you do too much of the same thing, *you* will be the one others will try to differentiate from, while you will end up blending into the normal and boring.

Note: A headline and subject line style should *never* be used if it doesn't fit your brand's tone and voice! It could cause more harm than good if applied this way. This warning actually applies to everything you do online, but it's worth mentioning here, as it's something many brands overlook when building articles or sending email communication.

EMPHASIS

When preparing visual assets, it is important to recognize which elements we want our users to notice and interact with first, and which of them are secondary and optional. Generally, our call to action elements will be those which we will want users not to lose sight of, and any headline or value proposition for this call to action will be where we want to draw our users' eyes towards first.

Three main ways we will be able to achieve this are:

1) Color: If you ever took an art lesson or two, you

may remember hearing about the color wheel, or at least some conversation about *Primary, Secondary, Tertiary,* and *Complementary* colors. Little did you know that these theories are essential to understand when presenting your offer online.

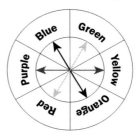

Look at the diagram on the right, which is a simplified version of the color wheel*. If you choose any color, the color on the opposite of the wheel will be its complementary color.

In your visual presentation, you will invariably have one color that dominates throughout; often times, it's the main color for your brand. The easiest way to make one element stand out from the others is to color it in the complementary of whichever is your dominating color. For example, if you have a website that is primarily blue, the complementary color is orange. This will be the color that will stand out the most against the primary.

You can also choose a color that is not exactly the complement of your dominant color, but rather right beside the complement on the color wheel, and the idea still works. In our example, you can choose a reddish-orange or a yellowish-orange, and it will still stand out against a dominant blue.

*Note: Digital media usually deals within the Red-Green-Blue (RGB) model and not Red-Yellow-Blue, but the latter model still works in digital. If you feel you must use an RGB model, by all means do so! The principle works in the exact same manner.

2) Contrast: On the other hand, you can make elements stand out by making sure they are in contrast with each other. For example, If your dominant elements are light, a darker element will most likely stand out, and vice-versa.

3) Form: Yet another way to ensure an element calls the attention of your audience is by placing it in a different shape than the rest of your presentation. For example, if 90% of your presentation is dominated by squares, in most cases, a hexagon or star element will probably stand out.

If you're able to stack all three tips (color, contrast, and form) onto your most important element, you can almost be certain that it will pop off the screen and attract your visitor's attention. This is also why digital presentations chock full of all different colors and shapes are unappealing and ineffective. The eye want to be guided towards the first, second, and third most important elements. Now you know the secret of how to achieve this through design.

You can read many more of my free articles and tips on how to stimulate the creative process here: www.cstps.co/creativity

Now that your assets have been produced, it's time to let them be seen and interacted with. Let's move on to our next phase, where we take all your assets live on the Web: *Distribution.*

CHAPTER V

Organized in Propagation
DISTRIBUTION PHASE

Every business owner and marketer knows that a solid distribution is essential. However, we often think about distribution methods only in terms of delivering products to our customers. While this is of great importance, delivering the message *about* our offer is as crucial, if not more important.

Think about it: How can you profitably deliver a product without an order taking place? And how do you initiate an order without informing a prospect about your offer?

Surprisingly, when it comes to sending an offer into the digital space, most businesses approach this process as an on/off function: It's not there, then one day, suddenly it's live.

In this chapter, I would like to challenge that notion a bit, and bring to your attention a few important details that will ensure your strategy doesn't fail due to bad distribution. A key to making your digital presence irresistibly attractive is not only *what* you present your audience with, but *how* you do it.

As in the previous chapters, you will need to adapt the information here to your particular offer and strategy. Take what works, leave what doesn't; but please, don't disregard a point just because something seems too unfamiliar. I can assure you that the details I speak about here are based on many years of experience distributing offers for global brands on the Web.

ORGANIZING ASSETS

Before you proceed to output and distribute online, take a look at your Strategy Blueprint and Required Assets list. Are all elements required to run the Strategy complete from top to bottom?

Organization is a huge requirement for our next phase, so we want to make sure that each asset is located in a place that is logical and useful: Logical, in that you and other team members will be able to predict with ease where each type of asset can be pulled from; and useful, in that the assets will not require any further effort to make them functional before we can distribute them.

If your strategy consists of several phases, we will want to create a separate directory for each phase, under which we will collect all assets pertaining to it. This will not only help us collect all files, but also assess quickly if any assets are missing or need to be modified.

We will then want to create subdirectories according to media type: graphics, audio, video, Web, etc. In general, we will want to keep source and project files under their own separate directories, and not jumble them with the output files. For example, Photoshop (PSD) files should be in one directory, and the compressed images we export from Photoshop will be in another directory at a higher level in the file structure.

Some people advocate creating directories for each file *format*, but I don't think this is very helpful. Remember, we're not trying to bow down to our computers. On the contrary, we're looking to create digital files that make sense to humans. Unless you need to place different file formats in separate directories, feel free to collect them in a way that makes sense to you. For example, if AIFF files make sense alongside MP3 files, so be it. On the other hand, if it makes more sense that JS files are organized separately from your CSS files — as is often the case — then that's the way to go.

FILE NAME CONVENTIONS

Part of being organized is to have a uniform way to name your files. There are many different naming conventions, and one might work better than the other in your particular situation. I won't waste time campaigning for the one perfect way to name your files, as I don't really have a strong stance on this, except for one guideline: Whatever you choose, **stick with it and be consistent!**

Naming your files according to 10 different conventions in one project can be very frustrating. Uniformity is more important than finding the one "perfect" way to name your files.

Here are a few general guidelines on how to name your files:

- Avoid special characters (#, $, %, etc.) unless absolutely necessary.
- Avoid spaces. Use underscore (_) or dashes (-) if needed.

- Lower-case or CamelCase is preferable over all UPPERCASE.
- File names should have only one period, right before the file extension (.css, .jpg, etc.)
- Whenever possible, 3-letter filenames are preferable over 4+ letters. For example, .mpg is preferable over .mpeg, .tif is better than .tiff, and so on.

Numbers indicating versions of a file should be reserved for source and project files, not for final output files, which in all likelihood will be written over many, many times. If an output file needs to be rolled back to a previous version, it's often easy to just output another file from an older source file.

Now that everything is organized, let's explain a few concepts about how to propagate our offer over the Web.

EARNED VS. OWNED VS. PAID MEDIA

When it comes to distribution channels, one of the fundamental distinctions to consider is between earned, owned, and paid channels. It would be a mistake to treat these channel types in the same manner, as each one has its own uses, challenges, and potential benefits.

Let's take a moment to discuss each one:

OWNED MEDIA

These are channels that, as the name clearly states, are owned and controlled by your company. Here you have the most flexibility to customize your message as much as you desire; therefore your most critical customer interactions will typically occur on this type of media.

Your website, e-commerce site, landing page, squeeze page, applications, branded games and experiences, among others, are all examples of owned media.

What about social media? When you have a company Page on Facebook, is that an example of owned media? To a degree, yes. These are spaces you can brand and verify so they are "official" extensions of your brand presence.

However, you will never be able to *fully* control these spaces. If Facebook decides to one day eliminate your company Page, they are certainly in their right to do so. For this reason, we can consider them as owned media, insofar as they are accessible and customizable by you. At the same time, due to the risk of it suddenly pulled outside of your control, I would advise against establishing these as critical touchpoints for your customers.

By critical touchpoints, I mean spaces where your audience makes a critical purchase decision, or executes the purchase itself.

You may find that some social media channels can be treated as *paid media* instead; so let's move onto the next category.

PAID MEDIA

These are channels that you pay to be present on and place your message in. For a fee, the channel may give up a degree of control, but more than likely the main value you will be looking for is direct and immediate exposure to that channel's audience. Typically, the greater the audience potential, the more expensive it will be to place your message on a particular paid channel.

Obviously, any advertising method is an easy example of paid media. Other examples are sponsorship avenues, and paid/sponsored messages driven by users' organic behavior, such as search, retargeting, etc.

In the majority of cases, you will leverage *paid media* to drive interest towards your *owned media*, and will not make paid channels your customer's final destination. For this reason, a clear call-to-action message on paid channels is a must.

EARNED MEDIA

Earned media are channels over which you have absolutely no control, but because of the success of your other brand efforts and your usage of owned and paid media, your offer is effectively distributed through them. Earned media can be the most powerful distribution channel for your offer, as the level of credibility that goes along with it cannot be compared to any other type of media.

The main example of earned media is word-of-mouth from your followers, fans, and customers. In other words, what people who have experienced your brand are currently saying about you. Word-of-mouth manifests itself through the digital realm in many forms: comments, reviews, posts, tweets, and overall conversation and buzz.

While you can't control these, the tactics and strategies in the previous chapter may help enable, influence, and monitor earned media.

SELECTING THE BEST CHANNELS

In your Strategy blueprint, you should have already selected the channels that supported your goals. Now that we've covered the difference between owned, earned, and paid channels, take a moment to re-evaluate your selected channels. More importantly, think about how your audience will move from one channel to another.

Keep in mind how control and credibility flow in opposite directions: The more control over a channel, the less the credibility in your audience's eyes, and vice versa.

Some of the best strategies will ignite a brand message through channels that grant a greater level of control, and will enable it to organically spill over into channels with a lesser level of control, yet higher level of credibility.

DISTRIBUTION FRAMEWORKS

One of the most essential notions about distribution that large brands understand is that human beings perceive messages *sequentially*, especially if they're composed of several big ideas. Unless you have only one shot to speak to your audience, it's recommended that big ideas be presented in phases, because in the end, this is how we experience the world around us. There is absolutely no scenario in the natural world in which we perceive an overload of information all at once. We focus on the first element that catches our attention, then move on to the next one in order of importance or appeal, and so on.

However, brands that deploy campaigns or experiences through digital media tend to blast every message they have all at once. This not only leaves audiences confused, but in the end, it also is a disservice to the message itself, as a good portion of it is left without being consumed at all, through nobody's fault, other than our inability as humans to process too much information at one time.

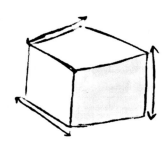

The three dimensions of a proper distribution breakdown are:

a) Time. It is just a simple fact that we process different ideas at different times. A famous philosopher once defined time itself as, "the succession of one idea after another in the mind." One of the most basic ways to compose your framework will be to distribute your big ideas at different periods.

b) Space. Naturally, we're talking about *digital* space here, and what we're referring to is spreading your big ideas over several different channels or media. There are many successful campaigns with the exact same content re-stated over different media, so that if the audience misses out on a portion of the message through one, it can pick it right up on the other.

Of course, the fact that a series of ideas is distributed over space, *also* necessarily means that it is perceived across a period time. However, we differentiate between the two, given that a distribution only in time may mean that it is performed in the same space but at different times.

c) Particularity. This dimension has to do with whether the idea is being distributed in general to any available audience as a whole, to just one member of the audience, or any segments of audience in between. Digital media has made it quite possible to segment audiences or even offer highly unique and personalized experiences to one individual audience member at a time.

Now that we know the "dimensions" in which a distribution takes place, let's discuss a few possible frameworks.

DIRECT FRAMEWORK

In this type of distribution, there really isn't that much expansion through either of the dimensions stated above. It's the typical framework used for something simple, like a landing page. Even though there's not much of a framework to speak about, we need to be aware that it is a type of framework that lacks expansion across any of the dimensions.

DRIP FRAMEWORK

As the name implies, this one "drips" information throughout a period of time. In most cases, a Drip framework will expand over the time dimension, while utilizing the same space. For instance, a sequence of emails, each one with a different big idea and delivered a different day of the week, is a typical example of a campaign within a Drip framework.

Parody singer Weird Al Yankovic used a drip framework for the promotion of his album "Mandatory Fun," for which he released a new music video each day for an entire week. This simple distribution idea helped him land on the very top among the best-selling albums of the year in a very short period of time.

EXPERIENCE FRAMEWORK

By spreading a message based over different phases of an audience's experience when interacting with a brand, you may be able to attain a higher level of relevancy in the audience members' eyes, while respecting the "distance" they have from your brand at certain moments.

One of the most popular segmentations of the Experience Framework is:

a) Know

b) Like

c) Trust

d) Try

e) Purchase

f) Refer

Your distribution plan will be spread out in time, space, and even particularity to correspond with each of these incremental states of the audience's familiarity with your brand.

RESPONSE-BASED FRAMEWORK

Whereas the Experience Framework is based on levels of familiarity with a brand, the Response-Based Framework looks at the reaction we desire to provoke from the audience at each stage. This framework can be segmented in this manner:

a) Awareness

b) Interest

c) Engagement

d) Expectation

e) Action

As in the Experience Framework, your distribution plan will be spread out in the three dimensions, corresponding to each of these targeted reactions in your audience. There is really no correct or incorrect distribution framework, so you should choose the one that best supports your goals and your Strategy Blueprint, adapting it as needed.

The only no-no here is to mix from different frameworks within the same Strategy. For example, you don't want to begin with an Experience Framework and then let go of it all and end with a Drip Framework approach. In the ideal scenario, for the sake of clarity and effectiveness, your message will begin and end within the same framework.

MANUAL VS. AUTOMATED DISTRIBUTION

Depending on the dimensions chosen for any tactic in your strategy, you might find that it's necessary for you to distribute manually and in real time. In other instances, you could set up an automated system to distribute for you.

Each one has its distinct advantages and disadvantages:

Manual. Examples: Uploading a file to a server,

replying to an email, live video broadcast, live chat, etc.

Pros: Complete control.

Cons: Time-consuming.

Automated. Examples: Autoresponders, scheduled-posting, custom feedback based on user input, etc.

Pros: Time-efficient.

Cons: Decreased control.

Your Distribution plan could very well have a blend of Manual and Automated processes. Make note of which method is used for which portions of your strategy, and look out for the potential problems when using each method.

The most frequent problem that occurs with automated distribution systems is when brands fail to implement a system to quickly stop or modify all tasks. You never want to be the brand that keeps peddling an offer while everyone is paying attention to a worldwide crisis. You and your team should share a list of automated tasks, along with the links, usernames and passwords to stop or modify them when those cases occur, because they *will* occur.

TRACKABILITY

One of the advantages enjoyed by digital media is the ability to track all sorts of aspects related to audience's behavior, and how they affect our strategy's performance. Back in the Strategy phase, we discussed the topic of defining our KPIs. In the phase right after this one (*Analysis*), we'll take a look at how to interpret the data to determine if those KPIs are met.

The bridge that connects these two points is to make sure that our assets are trackable, at a level that will allow us to measure them later on.

Usually, lines of code and/or small applications that are never perceivable by the general audience will be required on every asset in order for them to be trackable. Therefore, make sure these are present before taking anything live.

Let's talk about a few elements you should always consider in preparing for trackability.

LINKS

Generally, if anything important will be clicked, it probably should be tracked. One of the most foundational elements users click on are links. By the way, taps on mobile and other touchscreen devices are also commonly called "clicks."

Links can be constructed to include a surprising amount of data embedded in them, which will then be read and analyzed later by a separate application. In the case of links pointing towards the same destination, but placed in different locations, (separate pages, social channels, etc.) you may want to include different data on each placement — essentially making each one a different link. This way, you'll be able to track where that click came from, at which point in the strategy it was clicked on, and other valuable information.

For example:

http://digitalbaconbook.com/?utm_source=author&utm_medium=book&utm_campaign=example

http://digitalbaconbook.com/?utm_source=search&utm_medium=email&utm_campaign=promotion

While these point towards the exact same destination, these two links tell a completely different story about where the user came from, and what they were experiencing before being redirected. The first one tracks clicks from the book as an example, while the second one is more fit for a promotion via email.

In more advanced applications, you can dynamically change the data contained in these links based on user input and other external data feeds.

LANDINGS

Just as you can track stats about a user's origin, you should include code on every destination a user will arrive at. Your tracking code will be able to record many aspects of a user's behavior, and in some instances, even details about their origin can be discerned.

Probably the most popular tracking code, due to being free but also because of its breadth, is Google Analytics. You can sign up for free with a Google account at analytics.google.com. Once there, you can generate a tracking code and add it to each of your web properties.

Some examples of behaviors you will then be able

to track:

Number of views for each page

Number of unique visitors

Audience description

Traffic sources

E-commerce related behavior such as product views, shopping cart updates, etc.

EVENTS

As we drill deeper into user behavior, we might want to track more minute actions that a user takes on your properties. For example: Sharing, searching, zooming, printing, downloading files, video plays, and many others. These particular actions are more properly called "events," and as in the other cases, we must include a tracking code on any item the user interacts with to activate these functions.

The standard anatomy of an event tracking code will include three pieces of data:

Category: This describes what element the user is interacting with. Is it a button, a file, a video, or something else?

Actions: This speaks about what the user did with that element. Was it a download, a video rewind, a purchase?

Labels: This further identifies the event, as needed in your campaign. For example, if your strategy involves distributing three separate videos to users, the Category field by itself is insufficient information. With a label you'll be able to identify precisely *which* of the three videos the user interacts with.

GOALS

Your strategy will ideally lead towards one or more final desired actions on the part of your audience, which are often called "goals." You can also place a special code on the landing page or screen that represents that goal, to later track your success rate. The four types of goals are:

Destination: A page or screen that a user arrives at. Example: A "thank you for your purchase" confirmation page.

Duration: An amount of time that a user spends at a particular location. Example: More than 5 minutes reading content.

Pages/screens per session: A minimum number of pages/screens loaded by the user in a single experience.

Event: We already covered event tracking in particular, but an event also can be considered a final goal in your overall strategy. For example: a "share" or "subscribe" button, video play, etc.

THE ULTIMATE WEBSITE PRE-LAUNCH CHECKLIST

Before you launch a new presence on the Web, there are certain actions I **strongly** recommend you take to ensure that your site is compliant with search engines, and to guarantee there will be no technical issues in getting more prospects to connect with you.

On the following page is a handy checklist you might want to go through before taking a new site live. *You can also download it for free at* www.cstps.co/checklist. If you have a web designer/developer working for you, you can send this link directly to them.

☐ Sign up for Google Analytics (or another analytics engine) and ensure the code is present on each and every page of your site. You can find Google Analytics here: www.cstps.co/googleanalytics

☐ Make sure your site is registered and verified under Google Webmaster Tools (www.cstps.co/googlewebmaster), as well as Bing Webmaster Tools (www.cstps/bingwebmaster).

☐ Once your site is verified under these Webmaster Tools, have Google and Bing crawl it, and then return after a while to check for any errors that might come up. If you see any errors, fix them or hire someone capable to do it for you.

☐ If you are working on a Wordpress site, the SEO plugin I recommend is here: www.cstps.co/wordpressSEO.

☐ Make sure your website doesn't have any broken links. You can use this tool to easily check your entire site: www.cstps.co/brokenlinkchecker.

☐ Check your copy to see how readable it is. You can use this tool to do it quite easily: www.cstps.co/readablecopy

☐ Your title tags should ideally be 65 characters or less, while your meta description tags should remain at 155 characters or less. You can check the length of these very easily by using this tool: www.cstps.co/metalength.

☐ Ensure the primary keyword for each of the pages is in its URL. Dashes (-) are acceptable as separators between each keyword.

☐ Make sure your main keyword is on your page's

H1 tag.

- [ ] Do the images on your page have descriptive ALT tags? Make sure they do, as search engines read this data for indexing purposes.
- [ ] Make sure your site has no duplicate content, i.e.: The text content present on one page should not found in the exact same manner on another page.
- [ ] Measure your site's loading speed, and fix all errors. You can use this handy tool to do this: www.cstps.co/sitespeed.
- [ ] Include a sitemap for your website. You can generate one easily here: www.cstps.co/xmlsitemap.
- [ ] Create and upload a robot.txt file to the index directory of your website. You can generate this file easily here: www.cstps.co/robotstxt . You can create a temporary robots.txt file and refuse all search engines for a period, if your site will be uploaded but is still in development.

Register your brand on each of these sites. If for some reason your exact name is not available anymore, find something as close as possible.

- [ ] Twitter
- [ ] Facebook
- [ ] Yelp
- [ ] YouTube
- [ ] StumbleUpon
- [ ] Google+
- [ ] LinkedIn
- [ ] Wordpress.com
- [ ] Tumblr
- [ ] business.pinterest.com
- [ ] Instagram (may need to do from a mobile app)

- [ ] Make your site is ready to display structured data to search engines. Use this link to check your site

for structured data: www.cstps.co/structureddata
☐ Test your site on all the most popular desktop and mobile browsers. You can set up a testing lab, or you can do this for a significantly lower cost on this site: www.cstps.co/browsertesting. If you come upon any errors, fix them or hire someone to fix them for you before you go live.
☐ Install Google Authorship on your website. You can learn how to do this here: www.cstps.co/authorship .

NOTIFYING THE WORLD

No matter what content you are planning on publishing over the web, you will be competing for attention against *billions* of other pages, sites, videos, apps, etc. Knowing this fact, it's reasonable that an asset modestly placed online, without any proper effort to get noticed, will end up receiving a very poor number of visits and views. If your brand is not already massively renowned, you **must** make a concerted effort to lift your message above the noise.

The good news is that the tools to enhance your message are more accessible today than ever before, and in most cases, they are either free or very cost-effective. Let's look at some of the ways we can grab the world's attention! Or at the very least, your target audience.

PING

Whenever content is placed or updated online, it's often a good idea to let the search engines know that there is something they should take a look at. One way to do this is to log into every search engine and notify them, usually through a command called "ping" or "crawl". This can be awfully time-consuming, but fortunately there are services like that will notify a good number of sites with only one submission.

You can find one of these tools here: www.cstps.co/ping

POST

Sending a link to your content via your social sites is never a bad idea, and can be a quick and cost-effective way to get some initial traction on your content. The one guideline to keep in mind is to make sure your posts are not just a link and headline. They should feel organic, conversational, and befitting to the chosen social channel. Some examples and tips:

Twitter: Write a quick summary about the content, and then add the link and related hashtags, if any. If you can fit an image related to the content, that's often an attention-grabber.

Facebook: Add an image, and write some words inviting the audience to view or interact with the content. **Never type words asking for people to Like and/or Share**, as Facebook will absolutely crush your organic reach. A post with a photo and a link in the text area will typically perform better than a post with a link that will be styled the way Facebook usually does for all links.

Google+: Add a photo, or better yet, an animated GIF about your content. Start the post with a 4-5 word headline, with asterisks at the beginning and end of the line so it will appear in bold font. Write some introductory copy, then invite people to click the link to read more.

It's never a bad idea to let your close friends and associates know about your posts, so that they can help you amplify (through retweets, likes, shares, and comments) if they wish. You may also want to consider setting up a paid campaign on some of these channels to increase your reach and visibility.

PROMOTE

If your content is important enough, or in cases where you will derive direct monetary value from visits, you might find it useful to use paid channels to promote your content. Facebook promoted posts, Google AdWords, Sponsored Tweets and Yahoo/ Bing Ads are the channels I first look into, as they've performed well for me. However, there are many other paid channels to choose from.

HOW MUCH SHOULD YOU BID ON PAY PER CLICK ADS?

First, figure out — or estimate — your Conversion Rate. In other words, out of every 100 visitors, how many of them take the action you ultimately desire? We'll call this percentage your CR.

Now find out your Average Customer Value, or better yet, your Average *Lifetime* Customer Value. In other words, how much on average will one new customer bring in revenue for the duration of time they do business with you? Let's call this number ACV.

How much of that revenue will you devote to bringing this customer to you? 10%? 20%? Whatever percentage (%) you're comfortable with, multiply this number by your ACV, and then divide it by 100. In mathematical terms: $(ACV \times \%) \div 100$. Let's call this number your Maximum Spend per Customer, or MSC.

The formula I like to use is:

$$MSC \div (100 \div CR) = Max\ PPC\ bid$$

The resulting number is the maximum you should bid per click to attract visitors. In some cases, you may be surprised at how high this number is. However, if it's too low, you may need to either increase your CR — there are some tips on how to do this in the following chapter — or your ACV, via a higher price point, increasing retention rate, etc.

The great thing about figuring out your Max PPC bid using this formula is you can apply this knowledge towards other paid channels. You can review other Audience Building Tactics on page 93.

PARTNER

You may be able to collaborate with others who will help you promote your content for free, or for a reasonable incentive. A few ideas on ways to do this:

Outreach. Bloggers and online publishers are constantly looking for good content to promote. If your offer is compelling to their focus subject matter, they might be passionate enough to want to publish about it. If you can, give them an incentive that might support their goals in some way. For example, give them first dibs on a piece of news, create some content personalized to them while at the same time related to your brand, etc. You'll definitely want them to perceive that they're receiving more value than what you're getting back.

Affiliate. You may want to offer others a percentage of a sale whenever they send traffic to your offer, resulting in a conversion. There are many software packages and services that will allow you to create unique URLs for each of your affiliates, which will then track each purchase, enabling you to see which of your affiliates deserves the credit for that traffic.

Earned Media. We already talked about this one at the beginning of this chapter. Your offer might be so compelling, or your service so fantastic, that people feel glad to promote your brand. An extreme example is online communities like Slickdeals.com, where members gladly share heavily discounted offers they find, in turn sending server-crippling traffic to retailer's sites. Your strategy doesn't need to go that far, but you get the idea.

Simple good will. It's always a good idea to be good to others, without expecting anything in return. This includes promoting other people's content, brand, and offers for free. However, you may find that your goodwill pays off in such a way that people in your circles are more than glad to help promote and support you.

PUBLISH

The concept of "Content Marketing" is a really hot topic right now. Surveys suggest that more than 70% of users are driven towards purchase decisions and traffic in a more effective manner through good content than through advertising. Your web presence can include a strategy to publish content — whether written, graphic, audio, video, or some other format — that drives interest and action.

It's always a good idea to think about the audience first when developing content, and what *they* would want to consume. Remember that the goal here is to drive visits to your web property, and establish your brand as the right source to buy from, but you will want to achieve this indirectly by catering first to their already-existing interest.

Once your content satisfies their desire for information, it's totally fine to pitch your offer, unless there's such a smooth transition to reach out for your product or service that the pitch is no longer necessary.

Beware though: Online content can drive visits to your offer, but you might find that your content *itself* needs to be promoted as well. Content marketing is not a magic pill, and in most cases can take months to show significant results.

DESIGNING A DISTRIBUTION PLAN

Now that you have most of the main Distribution concepts in place, it's time to put them together into a comprehensive action plan. In order to do this, we're going to fill in a grid with each component of the distribution strategy. The axes of the grid will represent two of our three dimensions: time and space. We will have to repeat the same grid exercise for each segment of our particularity dimension.

You can download a Distribution Grid Template for free here: www.cstps.co/distributiontemplate

In the image above, you can see that at the top, we've established this distribution's Particularity as

"General Audience," which means that the assets in this strategy will be accessed by all Web users.

Right under this, we will clarify which Distribution Framework is being used. In this example, it's the Response-Based Framework.

The vertical axis is devoted to our time dimension, and as such is labeled with different time segments where a new asset in our distribution strategy will see the light. You don't have to begin with the exact dates at this point, those you can figure out later. Just choose a pivot event (such as, "launch day") and make all the dates relative to that pivot event (i.e.: "2 weeks before launch day").

The horizontal axis is our space dimension, and here we've laid out the different channels we plan on using.

Finally, on the bottom of our grid, right after each of the letters, we'll briefly list each of the assets required to run our strategy, one per letter.

Now, all we have to do is place our letters in the corresponding spaces on our grid. Plot everything out until all assets in your Strategy have been accounted for, and until your Distribution plan makes sense, particularly within your chosen distribution framework.

Once your Distribution plan is ready to deploy, and you've established a date for the pivot event, replace the spaces in the vertical axis with the actual dates. With this grid as your guide, publish these dates on a calendar accessible to you and your team.

By this point, we've gone through Discovery, Strategy, Production, and Distribution. Your irresistibly attractive web presence should be live by now! However, our BACON Process doesn't end here. In the next chapter, we'll go over the final — and very essential — phase of our process, *Analysis.*

CHAPTER VI

Numerically Measured

ANALYSIS PHASE

I'll be the first one to admit, I'm not a big fan of going to the doctor. Let me clarify: I am in no way minimizing the amazing work doctors perform. I just don't enjoy the process of calling to get an appointment, the waiting room with decade-old magazines, the awkward checkup process, and the co-pay checkout at the end through what feels like a cheap restaurant takeout counter. It was much more fun when you at least walked away with a lollipop!

Like many other people, I subconsciously avoid going to get myself checked up. This resistance is very similar to the way many businesses treat their web presence: They get everything up and running, and once it's live they never remember to seek a concrete report on how everything is performing.

But even with my own resistance to doctors, I have to recognize there is nothing quite like getting a diagnosis, blood test, etc., to set my mind at ease that everything is going well, or to determine correction opportunities for anything that may be going off course.

This is what our Analysis phase is all about.

Successful brands don't play around when it comes to metrics and analysis on their digital campaigns. This is their primary means to determine whether the resources invested produced any results. Furthermore, they measure with **numbers** (or other data derived from numeric values), which removes the analysis from the realm of subjective inter-pretation, and into concrete objectivity.

In this phase, we will perform a full check-up on our web presence, deliver a diagnosis, and determine enhancement and correction opportunities to make it stronger and healthier.

Your appointment is here. The nurse just called your name.

REVIEWING YOUR KPIs

Do you remember the Key Performance Indicators (KPIs) we established during our Strategy phase? Let's review them again at this point. If we were to extend the medical analogy, your KPIs would be akin to your vital signals. They will be the clearest indicator of what is going well, and whether anything is not going so well.

The first thing we need to do is pull up any metrics that existed before we began this process — that is, only if our offer *had* a web presence before we began, and we performed the exercises beginning on page 27. This will provide us with a historical data pool from which to judge from, even though I would dare to guess that now that you've followed a creative and strategic process, your results are bound to be dramatically better.

When reviewing your KPIs, the other question we need to ask is whether they were set at a realistic level. Was the scale too ambitious? Was the timeframe too aggressive? Were there other in-between milestones that needed to be met before reaching the KPIs? These are perfectly valid questions to ask, and in fact, *not* asking them could doom our process to failure unnecessarily. Remember: The first quality in our BACON Formula is *"Based on Reality,"* and we want to strive for nothing lower than that.

GATHERING THE DATA

This is where we'll refer back to all the elements we decided to make trackable back in our Distribution phase. If you did this successfully, you'll have a treasure-trove of data to record and analyze. We'll also have other data that didn't require us to install tracking codes, but are also available to us, such as number of subscribers, social following, and others.

At this point, we'll open a new spreadsheet, and label separate columns for the time periods. A column per month is suggested, but feel free to go more granular than that if you need to. In the first column, however, we'll place any target KPIs we had set during the Strategy phase. Let's label that column as "TARGET."

On each row, we'll place one of the metrics,

whether they're KPIs or secondary data. Make sure to record these figures as accurately as possible.

If your web presence just launched, and there were no pre-existing metrics, you will likely have enough data for the first column only. As we move forward, the other columns will be filled. We only need two columns to map out the tendencies, and our target KPIs vs. our actual KPIs will be a good starting point to analyze, even when we're at a very initial stage.

As our datasets grow, we can choose to visualize the data via line charts, pie charts, and all that fun stuff. Sometimes, it just helps to observe the tendencies in our data through a visual format.

You can download a Data Comparison Spreadsheet for free here: www.cstps.co/datacomparison. I recommend you fill this chart with a frequency that makes sense for your campaign.

INTERPRETING THE DATA

There is a huge difference between "metrics" and "analytics," though many people continue to be confused by thinking that data and analysis are one and the same thing.

In our situation, "data" will be just what we've been recording up to this point: Numerals describing the stats of our web presence. "Analytics," on the other hand, depend on *interpreting* that data. In essence, it's about figuring out what "story" our data are trying to tell us. In this process, we will be assigning *meaning* to what right now seem to be mere numbers and stats.

In order to do this, we have to continually refer to our original purpose for the digital effort, which should have been laid out clearly during our Strategy phase. All data should be interpreted in a way that communicates whether your purpose is being fulfilled or not.

A few methods for analyzing data that you can choose from are:

AVERAGE

Normally calculated by taking X number of data points, adding their numerical value, and dividing by X. For example, if we were interpreting visitation of a certain web asset, this would result in an average number of visitors during a certain timeframe.

DIFFERENCE

Here, we calculate the differences between separate points of data. In our example, we can express how much our visitation increased or decreased between one date and another.

FREQUENCY

We also can compare how frequently certain levels in our metric occur. For example, a drop in visitation every Saturday may point towards a pattern worth taking note of.

Of course, there are many other methods aside from these. What I recommend is, once again, to refer back to the original Strategy. If there are other interpretations required to evaluate success or failure, it just might be a matter of filtering the same data under a different method.

What are these interpretations telling you? In

the next few sections, we'll ask some more specific questions to not only help us analyze, but also take action on our findings.

IDENTIFYING WINS

It might be pretty obvious by now, but let's state it anyway: A win will be determined on the basis of a KPI meeting or exceeding our target. With the data and analysis we've performed up to this point, this should be pretty easy to point out.

Whenever we spot a win, it's important to identify which factors caused it, rather than just enjoying the sweet nectar of victory and forgetting about everything. Why? Well, if you have one win, we can only assume that several wins would be even better! The only way we can repeat a certain outcome is to determine the factors that brought it about and allow/cause them to occur again.

With regard to causes, here are some useful questions you can ask, while analyzing the data:

Was the win caused by a factor outside your control (like a seasonal surge of visits) or by a factor within your control (like an increased ad spend, which brought more visits)?

Was a certain component of the Strategy more effective than usual/expected? Why?

Have your earned channels expanded in scale and influence? Any particular reason?

If — and only *if* — you can place your finger on the exact factors that produced the desired result, then you will be able to do one of two things: a) Continue doing the same, or b) Increase what had been working well in your strategy.

Please note: There is really no guarantee that the same factors will produce the exact same results. There may be seasonal factors at play, the market in a certain area might be tapped out, your campaign could have a natural decline after losing its novelty, aside from any number of other possible reasons. However, by repeating or adapting to what you've determined *was* working correctly, at least you can make sure that any variances are not the result of the ignoring the successful factors in your Strategy, Production, and/or Distribution.

IDENTIFYING LOSSES

In the same way we identified wins, we will undoubtedly come upon instances where we will notice that results fell short of expectations. Depending on how much they fell short of what was expected, this may not be as bad of news as it may sound, as correction opportunities may be within our reach.

As in our previous exercise, when it comes to losses we also need to spend some of our efforts determining what were the exact factors that made our results fall short of our expectations. This is because we not only want to explore the possibility of correcting, but also the last thing we want is to spend our resources on something *other* than what needs to be fixed or improved. The same types of questions asked when identifying wins should be asked here as well.

Once the not-so-successful factors are identified, the possible solutions usually become quite apparent. To apply these solutions may cost additional resources, but it may be preferable to correct these specific areas, than to scrap the whole strategy developed up to this point.

Identifying wins and losses is one of the factors that separates successful online efforts from the rest. Don't overlook this essential phase!

OPTIMIZATION

Whether we're emphasizing winning aspects, correcting non-performing elements, or disposing of entire versions that don't work in exchange for others that do, the standard term for this effort is *Optimization*. This investment of resources is quite powerful, as it can help increase your revenue/performance while reducing costs.

The four main areas to look into when optimizing — among many others — are:

USER EXPERIENCE

By this point, you should have data on which pages and elements your users are interacting with the most, and also which of them are being found more easily. Are your assets clearly describing their purpose within your overall strategy? Is there a clear indicator ushering audience members towards the next action you want them to take? If there is anything that is confusing or driving users away from your intended action, or if there are any visual/copy amends that may help strengthen the call to action, take note of this and consider modifying these.

A great resource to test user experience with real, live human beings at an affordable price, can be found right here: www.cstps.co/usertesting

PERFORMANCE

You will want to measure how successful each element is in fulfilling its purpose from a functional point of view. For example, if a percentage of users is abandoning a shopping cart after placing items in it, is it because something on that page is not working properly? Or are there any language/visual cues that would help the user move forward with their purchase?

CONTENT

You will also want to consider whether your copy or visuals are compelling enough. Is your offer as clearly expressed as it should be? Every little element that a user comes into contact with may affect the performance of your campaign effort.

OFFER

If your digital effort is not compelling enough user action, it may be because your offer is not irresistibly attractive enough. You may be able to strengthen the attraction to your offer by either a) increasing the offer's perceived value, or b) decreasing the investment your audience needs to make in terms of time, money, or something else, to acquire your offer. On the other hand, even if your offer is already being acquired, you may be able to optimize your revenue by increasing the price/investment, decreasing your costs, or both.

> As mentioned in an earlier chapter: I've written an article titled *How To Make Your Offer Irresistibly Attractive*, which you can find here: www.cstps.co/oia

A/B TESTING

What if the exact causes of the wins and losses are not as easy to identify? In that case, we might want to perform what is commonly called an A/B Test, also known as split testing.

> For his second presidential campaign, President Obama raised an additional $60 million through the exact same campaign, by implementing A/B testing effectively.

The idea behind an A/B Test is deploying the exact same component of our strategy twice, with only one minor element of difference between them, this way creating an A version and a B version. This singular element of difference will be what we'll be examining. It could be a creative component, such as a headline, a photo, or a certain aspect of the layout. It could also be a structural element, like an element that affects load time. Whatever it is, we want to make sure *only one* element is different each time we run the test.

Then, through a script or software application, we will split our traffic, and randomly send half of our audience to the A version, and the other half to the B version, making sure that we'll be able to report our findings at a later date. Whichever version performs the best is the keeper. If it's necessary to continue testing — and you should be testing continually! — we'll take the winning version, and once again split it into two with another element of difference.

Three of the most popular platforms to achieve this are Google Content Experiments (within Google Analytics), www.cstps.co/vwo, and www.cstps.co/optimizely, but there are many others as well.

MULTIVARIATE TESTING

Similar to A/B testing, Multivariate Testing splits your traffic among several properties, only in this instance, a larger number of differences is acceptable at one time, rather than just two.

The advantage of this method is that you are able to get a clear picture of how several elements perform at any one time. However, this method typically requires a very high amount of traffic in order for it to offer valuable insight. The advantage is that you will be able to measure the effectiveness of many elements during one single test deployment. In any case, I strongly recommend sticking to A/B Testing as much as possible, especially during the initial periods after the Distribution phase, when you may still be building your traffic slowly.

ALWAYS BE TESTING!

As I mentioned at the beginning of this chapter, you will want to have complete knowledge about how your digital effort is performing. There are no *perfect, one-shot efforts.* There are *always* details we can improve, issues we can fix, and modifications that will produce better results for our businesses.

The only way to achieve this is to continually run through our Analysis tasks, which will in turn shed light on whether we need to repeat any tasks from one of our previous four phases. Here are some examples:

Discovery: We may need to run deeper research into our market, or explore a new market to help us continue growing.

Strategy: We may encounter the need to modify our strategy, deploy a new one altogether, or aim towards a different primary KPI.

Production: Our Analysis may show that we need to modify some of our assets, or create new ones.

Distribution: We might need to deploy our assets under a different framework, or re-deploy new assets created through different channels.

Make no doubt about it: If you decide to return to one of the previous phases *without* the proper analysis, you're opening your business up to wasted resources. On the other hand, with our analysis guiding us, we can confidently return to strengthen our previous phases in a continuous and informed manner.

And that's it!

Congratulations on implementing all five phases and going for the BACON! However, the journey doesn't end here...

Closing Thoughts

In this book, I've given you a detailed overview — as detailed as I can — of how the Digital BACON Formula works when applied to a digital effort that really sizzles. There is simply no way that I can describe every detail and nuance of the Digital BACON Process in one single book, but I trust that what you have read so far has given you many practical lessons that you can apply to your digital presence immediately. These will help you grow your business in a dramatic fashion by using digital technology available today.

As you can see from the last section in my previous chapter, the five phases resulting from our Digital BACON Formula are meant to be *cyclical*. In other words, this formula is by no means a linear pipeline where we come in from one end and out through the other, while everything continues to run on autopilot.

Renowned brands all around the world that put forth the most successful digital campaigns — including Disney, Adidas, AXE, RedBull, and countless others — understand that the five elements in the Digital BACON Formula are not only what produce an irresistibly attractive presentation of their offer, but also what *sustains* this presentation, and allows it to remain successful throughout extended periods of time. Regardless of whether they call their process by this name or not, you will find these five qualities present in every case study of the most successful digital efforts, and in a manner in which they continuously dedicate resources towards strengthening themselves.

In no way am I pretending that incorporating the Digital BACON Formula is an easy task to accomplish in your business. It truly takes efforts, resources, and focus. What I *am* affirming, without a shred of doubt, is that this formula has proven itself as a worthwhile and profitable investment, while striving for anything less results in expenses without purpose.

You may want to use this book, along with the recommended materials, templates, worksheets, and resources, as a guide for you and your team in your digital efforts. I would be absolutely honored to learn that you've applied this system to achieve unparalleled results in your business.

However, you might feel like you need a bit of help to reach the five qualities in the Digital BACON formula.

If so, let's talk! Write me an email to my personal address at alex@ymmymarketing.com, and let's schedule a free 30-minute consultation to discuss which of these steps your business needs help with, as well as some solutions that can work for you.

We've applied this formula to large brands, as well as small- and medium-sized businesses, and even startups — some of them my own! I would personally enjoy nothing more than standing together with your organization, and witnessing yet another case study on how this powerful formula works to grow your bottom line and transform your brand.

Learn more about YMMY, my Digital Agency, at www.ymmymarketing.com

Let's get cooking!

Resources

Here's a list of all the links I recommended throughout the book. This will help you quickly look up anything you might have missed, or decided to leave for later.

Discovery Phase
- ☐ Discovery Worksheet: www.cstps.co/DiscoveryWorksheet
- ☐ How to Make Your Offer Irresistibly Attractive: www.cstps.co/oia
- ☐ How To Easily Perform a Competitive Analysis: www.cstps.co/competitiveanalysis

Strategy Phase
- ☐ Strategy Worksheet Link: www.cstps.co/StrategyWorksheet
- ☐ Traffic Estimate: www.cstps.co/trafficestimate
- ☐ Compete: www.cstps.co/compete
- ☐ Open Site Explorer: www.cstps.co/opensiteexplorer
- ☐ AHrefs: www.cstps.co/ahrefs
- ☐ Majestic: www.cstps.co/majestic
- ☐ Alexa: www.cstps.co/alexa
- ☐ Quantcast: www.cstps.co/quantcast
- ☐ Facebook Ad Manager: www.cstps.co/facebookads
- ☐ Pay With a Tweet: www.cstps.co/paywithtweet
- ☐ Wendy's campaign: www.cstps.co/pretzelsong

Production Phase
- ☐ Coggle: www.cstps.co/coggle
- ☐ Freemind: www.cstps.co/freemind
- ☐ XMind: www.cstps.co/xmind

- [ ] How To Produce Your Assets:
  www.cstps.co/howtoproduceassets
- [ ] Creativity articles: www.cstps.co/creativity

Distribution Phase
- [ ] The Ultimate Pre-Launch Checklist:
  www.cstps.co/checklist
- [ ] Google Analytics: www.cstps.co/googleanalytics
- [ ] Google Trends: www.cstps.co/googletrends
- [ ] Google Webmaster Tools:
  www.cstps.co/googlewebmaster
- [ ] Bing Webmaster Tools: www.cstps/bingwebmaster
- [ ] Yoast SEO: www.cstps.co/wordpressSEO
- [ ] Broken Link Check:
  www.cstps.co/brokenlinkchecker
- [ ] Copy Readability Test: www.cstps.co/readablecopy
- [ ] Meta Length: www.cstps.co/metalength
- [ ] Site Loading Speed: www.cstps.co/sitespeed
- [ ] XML Sitemap Generator: www.cstps.co/xmlsitemap
- [ ] Robots.txt generator: www.cstps.co/robotstxt
- [ ] Structured Data Checker:
  www.cstps.co/structureddata
- [ ] Cross Browser Testing:
  www.cstps.co/browsertesting
- [ ] Google Authorship: www.cstps.co/authorship

Analysis Phase
- [ ] Ping tool: www.cstps.co/ping
- [ ] Distribution Grid Template:
  www.cstps.co/distributiontemplate
- [ ] Data Comparison Spreadsheet:
  www.cstps.co/datacomparison
- [ ] User Testing: www.cstps.co/usertesting
- [ ] A/B Testing Tools: www.cstps.co/vwo &
  www.cstps.co/optimizely

ABOUT THE AUTHOR

Alex Rodríguez (🐦@AlxRodz) is a Creative Digital Marketer who develops high-end digital campaigns for successful businesses looking to transform their brand and grow their business further.

Throughout almost two decades of professional experience, he has created some of the most successful launches for global brands and products, most of which have resulted in millions of dollars in sales in record periods of time.

Alex has created strategic digital content for clients in 4 different continents and 3 separate languages (English, Spanish, and Mandarin).

As a result of his strategic creative, he has been honored with some of the most distinguished awards in Web, Advertising, and Social Media.

Alex heads up the team at YMMY Marketing (**ymmymarketing.com**), a digital creative agency in Florida, USA.

He often writes about how to strategically attract audiences at **www.CreativeStrategyTips.com** .

Alex is also the host and producer of *The Digital Marketing Minute*, a daily podcast.

CPSIA information can be obtained at www.ICGtesting.com
Printed in the USA
LVOW06s1248020914

402005LV00006B/16/P